The Imperfect Disciple

THE IMPERFECT DISCIPLE

Samuel Southard

BROADMAN PRESS · Nashville, Tennessee

422-510
Second Printing

Dewey Decimal Classification Number: 248.4
Library of Congress catalog card number: 68–20686
Printed in the United States of America
2.068KSP

To the people of God in the Fort Mitchell Baptist Church and to the servants of God in the ministers' workshop, Christ Hospital, Cincinnati, who heard and helped to revise the thoughts contained in this book

PREFACE

There may be some persons who are naturally lovable, who spontaneously seem to care for every person they meet, who seem untouched by temptation and trial.

If so, this book is not for them.

This book is for people who know they make mistakes. And, more is meant by the admission of "mistakes" than was acknowledged by the defensive husband who yelled, "All right, all right, so I make mistakes, but being wrong is not one of them!"

This book is for conspicuous sinners, secret failures, inadequate individuals, lustful and power-driven leaders —for anyone who knows for sure that he is not a perfect disciple.

It is written for people who are troubled by their inadequacies, who cannot love the unlovable, and who know who some of the unlovable ones are!

These are the people who turn to Christ as their only hope, for they know the limitations of their love and obedience.

CONTENTS

The Imperfect Disciple

1

Discipleship Despite Limitations

We deceive ourselves when we think that our judgments and decisions are absolute. History has a way of making them look foolish. One satirist, writing in *The Christian Century* (Feb. 10, 1965), found that Moral Rearmament had taken a stand for "absolute honesty." But one of their spokesmen was smearing the moral standards of the United States diplomatic service in Latin America. Even as he made sly, insulting insinuations about homosexuality in Mexico City, he also said that he hated "the public assassination of character." By his own judgment, he was judged.

The satirist also recalled that in the 1930's Frank Buchman, a founder of MRA, had said, "I thank God for a man like Adolf Hitler." His "absolute" decision does not look so good thirty years later. The article concluded: "Isn't it fun for those of us who are only relatively honest, pure, unselfish, and loving to read how the other half lives?"

We cannot call ourselves perfect. As Jesus told a lawyer: "Why do you call me good? There is none good but God." Despite his sinlessness, our Lord rejected holy assurances and was a model of humility.

If the imperfections, the limitations of personality are taken seriously, we cannot speak of "perfect obedience," "total commitment," "absolute honesty," "complete perfection" in this life. What, then, can we strive for?

Commitment the Supreme Loyalty

Christian discipleship requires that a limited individual be motivated by the spirit and life of Christ. The Christian lives under principles of conduct that surpass the ways of natural man. Christ alone is perfect. Any perfection *we* may attain will be achieved by single-minded devotion, commitment to him as the supreme loyalty of life. Incomplete, inadequate people that we are, we still can find abundant life in Christ's call to discipleship, "Come, learn of me." In responding to his call, we find our completeness.

Two pairs of brothers were in their boats when Jesus passed near them on the shore and said: "Follow me" (Matt. 4:18–22). Later, he issued the same command to a tax collector (Luke 4:27–28). Others were engaged in occupations unknown to us when the Lord called them to be his witnesses (Luke 10:1ff.).

All these men were called to *become* disciples. A disciple is a learner. Jesus said, "By this my father is glorified, that you bear much fruit, and so prove to be my disciples" (John 15:8). This means much more than blind obedience or impetuous imitation. Jesus puts before men an ideal, a delayed honor for which they are to labor and yearn. His call is to a life of obedient service.

After instructing his twelve disciples, the Master declared: "Come to me, all who labor and are heavy-laden, and I will give you rest. Take my yoke upon you, and learn from me; for I am gentle and lowly in heart, and you will find rest for your souls. For my yoke is easy, and my burden is light" (Matt. 11:28–30).

New learning is a lifelong challenge and a part of the total meaning of discipleship. Eduard Schweizer[1] examined the many passages in which Jesus challenged men to follow him and has offered the following summary:

1. Obedience to Jesus' call of allegiance is the decisive act in the life of a man.

2. This call begins a new life for the believer.

3. "Follow me" means togetherness with Jesus and service to him.

4. Allegiance to Christ takes precedence over all other ties. A person may have to give up occupation, friendly relations with parents or kin, or even life itself to fulfil discipleship.

5. The way of Christ led to rejection, suffering, and death. This also may become the way of those who follow him.

In the *New Testament*, the word "disciple" is used (with one exception) only in the Gospels and Acts. The word "discipleship" is not used in the Gospels, although the writings are full of its meaning as a living reality. There is little biblical emphasis upon psychological analysis or rules for compliance. Instead, discipleship is a way of life in association with Christ. From the beginning of his ministry (Mark 1:18–20) to his resurrection appearances (John 21:19), discipleship is implied in the command of Jesus: "Follow me."

This command is a challenge, all the aspects of which are yet unknown. But many characteristics of a disciple are presented by the Lord, as in the Beatitudes (Matt. 5:3ff.). Instead of a set of rules, Christ gave men a gift that distinguishes them as disciples. This gift is salvation, and it imparts the spirit of Christ to a follower. By the guidance of the Holy Spirit, the believer will be led in all things.

However, the Counselor's guidance does not lessen the disciple's need for the example of the historical Jesus; for, discipleship is intimately connected with the attitudes of Jesus and the fate he suffered because of the response that some people made to him (Matt. 10:24f.; Luke 14:25–33). Futhermore, the disciple is to imitate his master. As Jesus served his followers, so they should humbly devote themselves to others (John 13:12ff.; Luke 22:24–26; Mark 9:33–37; Matt. 23:10–12).

Discipleship was to be distinguished by the way the disciples loved one another (John 13:35). The disciple would show in his attitudes and relationships the same qualities which Jesus manifested toward friends and enemies alike.

The high demands of such a life cannot be met by men in their own strength. Only as men are drawn to

God through Christ do they experience power to love the unlovely as he did (John 6:44ff.). For men, with all their limitations, can seldom give heartfelt affection to one another. Natural dislikes, cultural prejudices, personal wounds—all prevent the full flow of creature love. But by the power of God, men can desire good even for those who do them ill; they can act with love and justice toward others for whom they feel no intimate concern. A disciple is continually learning how to be like Christ. He has not yet attained; he is not yet perfected.

The supreme joy of discipleship is experienced in fellowship with Christ and in praise of God. Human friendship is the imperfect channel through which this fellowship and praise are often realized, but it is not the source. The ultimate goal of a disciple is not to love others and to be loved by them; rather, it is to love *God* as he loves us. From this will flow the love and respect for saints and sinners that should characterize the Christian disciple.

Knowledge of Imperfections

Discipleship demands self-knowledge. Without it, there is inadequate knowledge of God; and without knowledge of God, there is equally inadequate knowledge of self. One cannot answer God's *personal* call without becoming aware of himself. Called by God, Abraham saw himself as dust and ashes. (Gen. 18:27).

Knowing ourselves before God involves an awareness of both our possibilities and our limitations. So long as we live within our limitations as human beings, we are not condemned. The requirements for God's approval are clearly indicated in Micah 6:8:

> He has showed you, O man, what is good;
> and what does the Lord require of you
> but to do justice, and to love kindness,
> and to walk humbly with your God?

It is no sin to be human. We have been created by God. The Creator does not despise his creation. He has given us dominion over the works of his hands (Psalm 8:6). We are made in the very image of God (Gen. 1:27). As the highest being of his creation, man is capable of knowing God and of knowing himself.

But it seems that we cannot live as creatures with limitations. Instead, we rebel against the God who has made us and trample upon our highest endowment—the capacity for fellowship with God. The lament of our Creator is: "I have seen this people, and behold, it is a stiff-necked people" (Ex. 32:9).

We become sinners, not by the mere transgression of ethical codes, but primarily by refusing the divine-human relationship. Isaiah speaks the cry of Jehovah:

> Sons have I reared and brought up,
> but they have rebelled against me.
> The ox knows its owner,
> and the ass its master's crib;
> but Israel does not know,
> my people does not understand (1:2-3).

Our unwillingness to live as God's creatures alters

our inner nature. Instead of growth as children of God, we distort our nature by self-worship. Created to know ourselves by knowing God, we forsake the Creator and become the foolish selves that Paul describes: "Claiming to be wise they became fools, and exchanged the glory of the immortal God for images resembling mortal man" (Rom. 1:22–23).

We are blinded to our imperfections because we no longer regard our Heavenly Father's standard for measure and judgment. Then, as we seek to defend our inadequacies and excuse our mistakes, pride compounds itself. How shall we respond to the accusations of others that we are imperfect, or to the uncomfortable inner awareness that we cannot really do all things rightly?

Some people have succumbed to their inadequacies. Like the seed that falls upon the path, they are trodden under feet of men. For a lifetime thay have been treated as less than human. Opportunities for adequacy have never been presented to them.

Knowledge of imperfections is known early by some children. One schoolteacher said that his poorer children know by the third or fourth grade that they are only tolerated by middle-class children. "They made the mistake of being born to the wrong parents in the wrong section of the country, in the wrong industry, or in the wrong racial or ethnic group." [2] Motivation for achievement is greatly diminished, and in some of these children it seems to be extinguished.

But even in better economic or social circumstances, a person may still feel inadequate. Continual psychological deprivation can stifle the desire for independence. Consider the plight of one young man who had no incentive toward marriage, work, or self-respect. He did not know his father. He was raised by relatives who often reminded him that he was inferior. His hopes for a better life in school were dashed by teasing classmates. In late teens he "drifted" into the company of a homosexual and, after a time, was arrested with him. Three years later, in a state mental hospital, he would only shrug his shoulders when asked what he would like to do. Persons who have been abandoned, abandon hope themselves. "What's the use?" they say.

Other persons are less compliant. They conceal their inadequacies as best they can. Sometimes this is done by blaming others. Wife, husband, parents, friends, associates may be used to explain mistakes that actually originate in the deceptive person. He himself cannot say: "I did it." In his inner thoughts, he believes this to be a hostile world. Everyone is against him. If he admits anything, enemies will "do him in."

Very intelligent persons keep up this deception by excessive rationalization. A deacon or pastor may say: "We are to love our enemies, I know—and I *know* my enemies. All I am doing is protecting myself against what they would do to me. I get them before they get me. I wish they would let me love them."

Along with psychological deception, there is the great concealing power of the body. A wife *pretends* that she is happy when domineering in-laws visit, but her blood pressure goes up until she is hospitalized for dizziness. A mother seems to have a heart attack when she hears that an idealized child is going to marry. Consciously she says: "Oh, I wish this hadn't happened. Now I know my son won't marry—until I am well." A "self-made" man boasts that nothing ever gets under his skin. Yet all the while his mouth or eye muscles move nervously, or he bites his nails to the quick.

Why continue the deception—psychological or physical?

The Christian message is that all of our inadequacies, faults, failings, and sins are already recognized by God. And, while we are yet sinners, he has provided forgiveness through his Son. Why, then, continue to live under condemnation?

The best help for mistakes and failures is open confession to God as we become increasingly honest with ourselves. New hope and aspiration come from God and arrest the drifting that despair causes. We can face God's majesty and holiness and admit that all our pretended righteousness is nothing before him. Then we feel the impact of his love through Christ and are secure enough to admit our limitations. God will not condemn us if we trust him.

Imperfect human beings, lost from God in their rebellion, are restored to true selfhood when Christ lives within. Paul proclaimed: "I have been crucified with Christ; and it is no longer I who live, but Christ who lives in me; and the life I now live in the flesh I live by faith in the Son of God, who loved me and gave himself for me" (Gal. 2:20).

The confession of limitations is one stage in our new selfhood. Faith in Christ makes us children of God by adoption, family members with all those in God's household (Eph. 2:12–21). Our real selves are now set free to serve a living God (Gal. 4:1–11). Defenses and fantasies of grandeur are no longer necessary. As forgiven persons, we can grow into true maturity, because we are growing up into Christ, who is the chief cornerstone. With that kind of security, we can admit who we are.

The model for growth as a Christian person is Jesus Christ. Growth in Christian character is nourished both through the reality of the historical Jesus and through personal commitment to the leadership of the Holy Spirit.

The historical reality of Jesus is clear in the Gospels. The disciples believed that, as bearers of the good news, they were to walk in the way that Jesus had demonstrated before them. To know God and his will was to know Christ and his way of life, for his life was molded by obedient thought and action to the form of his father's pleasure. As his life was in imitation of God, so the life of a disciple would be an imitation of Christ (John 5:19; 13:20; 14:6). The theme may be summarized in 1 John 4:17: "As he is so are we in this world."

At the same time, the disciple knows that he cannot be above his Lord. There was only one divine Son of God. Therefore, any emphasis upon walking in Jesus' way must also include an understanding of the significance for our lives of his saviourhood, his divine mission, his death and resurrection. The apostle Paul and others reflect this thought in their use of the phrase "the mind of Christ."

This phrase emphasizes the qualities of character that were revealed in him—gentleness, humility, obedience, and suffering. Our lives are to show forth these spiritual qualities that were seen in Jesus Christ (2 Cor. 10:1; 13:4; Rom 15:3; Phil. 2:5–8; 1 Cor. 4:11; Eph. 4:32 to 5:2; 1 Peter 4:1,13; Heb. 4:15; 5:9).

The four Gospels and Paul's writings teach us how Jesus lived as a man and that, by the power of the Holy Spirit, a measure of the divine quality of his life can be had in our relations with God and man.

Growth in Grace

To set forth the ideals of Christian discipleship without recognizing human frailty only discourages the earnest disciple. Drs. Fairchild and Wynn found in their study of literature on the Christian family that many parents who read the material were more discouraged than before.[3] Some parents felt that they could *never* have the talent or faith exhibited by the model, middle-class families in certain denominational periodicals. Nor could they foresee simple answers in a short period of time, like the printed stories which solved complicated problems in four pages. The following chapters are meant to offer realistic understanding and encouragement for Christian growth in grace.

The disciple *is* to "grow in every way" like Christ. His will is to be the supreme loyalty of our lives. But we are still human, and this loyalty must be maintained in the midst of many other desires which still remain with us (chap. 2).

The virtues of loyalty, honesty, and integrity depend upon an enlightened mind. Long training is necessary to see things honestly and clearly in God's light (chap. 3).

Although we may strive for perfection, our personal devotional life will soon reveal that faith and virtue are in God alone. We do not even know how to pray as we ought. There is a mixture of primitive and prophetic worship in our lives (chap. 4).

Our conduct as disciples is to be patterned after the ways of Christ. We cannot know how to do this of ourselves, but he teaches a new piety to those who follow him (chap. 5).

A more realistic acceptance of who we are, including an understanding of our attempts to deceive ourselves, must be achieved. An analysis will be made of our selective inattention to Christ's command, of our desire to play games and pretend to be someone whom our inner self really denies (chap. 6).

Jesus knew how people would misinterpret his ministry and dissimilate discipleship. But he continued to teach his followers the meaning of repentance and forgiveness. Those who follow Christ have a right to be real people; they need no longer pretend (chap. 7).

Most important, Jesus taught: "If any man would come after me, let him deny himself and take up his cross and follow me. For whoever would save his life will lose it, and whoever loses his life for my sake will find it" (Matt. 16:24–25). There is a discipline in discipleship that distinguishes love from sentimentality, self-respect from self-indulgence (chap. 8).

2

Commitment to Discipleship

An executive, discussing a young man who was an employee said, "I think that this is a man who could have a great future. He looks good, he speaks well, he has a delightful family. When I tell him to do something, he gets it done the right way. But, I am not sure about where he stands on anything. I mean, if I send him out to a branch office, what does he represent? If someone from another division of our company is in a staff meeting and has a different idea from the one I have, with which one will my young man agree? I think he is living pretty much for his own success. I hate to say this, but I don't see him committed to anything."

The word "commitment" confronts many people in our very successful society who are continually tempted to get what they can for themselves in ways that will be approved by others. It is a special problem for "good people." They have had some measure of success in life, are surrounded by pleasant, fairly well-to-do neighbors, have not led riots or destroyed property, have not fallen into sins so grave that they are publicly disgraced.

Where is spiritual concern in the midst of such situations? We can hide our minor vices, we can gloss over some of our sins, but how are we going to answer the question raised by this branch manager: Is this man committed?

Characteristics of Commitment

Commitment means to live for something beyond ourselves, for something that endures.

The poverty-stricken person, collapsed in despair, is preoccupied with the problem of earning his daily bread. He has little time to think of anything beyond existence today. But what about the person of resources—one who earns a good salary, who is able to get what he wants? What does *he* live for? He has enough to eat. He has enough to clothe himself. He is able to buy the necessities of life. What beyond that?

Most of us can remember a brief period of time when we were greatly preoccupied with some particular fancy. But we would hardly use the word "commitment" to describe the temporary enthusiasm we felt about that one project. Often when boys are in little league teams, whole families are very enthusiastic about sports during the time the boy is playing. The children know that they are playing a game and are having fun. But occasionally, parents take it so seriously that some of them up in the stands have to be calmed down. The parent who stands up and screams, "That's my boy!" is certainly showing a kind of commitment. He is not just watching a child play ball, he is expressing a relationship in life with him. The enduring commitment (we hope) is to the child, not just to his thrilling moment of achievement on the ball field.

Sometimes, modern people wonder how to understand something like commitment because, for persons in many parts of society, there is no self-identification. They are just part of a company, part of a race, part of a neighborhood, or a state. If someone were to say, "What do you stand for?" such a person might have to think quite a while about what was meant by the question and about his answer.

"Identification" has now become a very elusive term. In 1860, Robert E. Lee was in Texas when that state overrode the objections of Sam Houston and sided with South Carolina and Alabama to join the Confederacy. Colonel Lee was told to surrender United States property under his command. He promptly replied, "I am an officer of the United States and a Virginian. I do not take orders from Texans!"

A few months later, Lee identified himself with Virginia against the United States. It was a part of his code of honor to protect family and state. This identification was too narrow, but it is an example of how men of previous generations could decide who they were. They were "Virginians," "Texans," "planters," "workmen," "free men," "slaves."

Many of these distinctions are blurred today, so blurred that people find religion is about the only way they can identify themselves. Professor Will Herberg of Drew University maintains that "Protestant," "Catholic," "Jew" are more cultural than spiritual designations in our society. If a man isn't in one of these three groups, then who is he? There is little self-realization in identification as broad as Herberg mentions. We must consider, therefore, another identification that can challenge our loyalties.

Commitment is a willingness to risk ourselves in openly declared allegiance. When Jesus said to his disciples, "Follow me," it was a call to break from the crowd and to become men who would walk away from the crowd in his presence. This decision is pressed upon every Christian. In one way or another we must stand up and be counted. In a Baptist church at the close of a sermon, a person who is moved by God's spirit walks down the aisle and is seen before men as one who has dedicated his life to Jesus Christ. Why is this done? Certainly, it is not because the one who comes is a great sinner who must be seen by the saints. Rather, this person is publicly proclaiming his belief in Jesus Christ, and thus he glorifies God.

This open identification must continue far beyond a church ceremony. It means that in school, or in a place of business, the person will stand up and say what he believes about Jesus Christ and will try to explain his faith in the Saviour to another. When there is a serious crisis, a time when speech is needed, Christians must be willing to identify themselves with their Lord.

A boy in junior high school liked his woodwork teacher very much although he, himself was no good at woodwork. But his teacher was, and the boy admired him. Even though the boy never expected to be a cabinet maker, he liked crafts because of his teacher who was a good man. One day the supervisor of the city schools made an inspection tour and looked at some samples of the boys' work in that class. He began to reprimand the teacher.

"This is sloppy work, and you are a poor teacher. You are letting them get by with all kinds of defects in their workmanship. If you were a real teacher, you wouldn't let this happen," he said.

All this was said in a side room, but the boys could hear it. As the supervisor came out, one thirteen-year-old young man walked up to him and spoke.

"Sir, I hope you got to know our teacher, because we think he's wonderful." The supervisor stopped, and the boy went on: "You know, I'm not very much of a carpenter. And, I'll never be a cabinet maker. I don't think I'll ever be much better at woodwork, but I'll always respect those who are because I respect our teacher who is a fine man. I hope you know this, too."

"Well, young man, thank you very much," the supervisor replied. "I appreciate this."

He looked around and saw that all the other boys felt the same way. Taking the teacher by the arm, they walked out into the corridor.

"Now, I'm sorry that I judged you the way I did," he apologized. "I was looking at this only from one point of view. If your boys stand up for you, I guess you've done something with them."

This quality of commitment—loyalty—prompts the Christian to take risks for the sake of a prized relationship, to speak well for his Lord when others have not seen him as they do.

Loyalty to Christ is the prime characteristic of Christian commitment. In the *person* of Jesus Christ are defined the values to which we are committed. His qualities become our goals in life. In him we can fulfil the requirements of commitment: service to someone beyond self; an enduring, steadfast relationship; open identification of allegiance; willingness to risk ourselves for the one who has given himself for us.

Mixed Motivations

This kind of loyalty does not depend on human strength or goodness. It is God who provides steadfast love and divine righteousness. All that is asked of man is that he fix his life upon one thing—loyalty to Christ. This, Jesus said in many parables, is the pearl of great price, the leaven in the lump, the good seed that grows and produces much fruit (Matt. 13).

But this loyalty must exist along with other motivations. The wheat grows among tares, the seed must live and mature among weeds and sometimes in hard ground.

What are some motivations that strive for dominance over Christ's claim upon our lives? Jesus dramatized some of them in his conversations with three men, as Luke records them in chapter 9 of his Gospel.

Divine call strives with human need for the security that ownership of property offers. One man wanted to follow Jesus wherever he went. Jesus reminded him that he had no earthly dwelling place. Because pride of ownership by inheritance, love for the soil, and dependence upon it for a livelihood were deep-rooted in Eastern life, the man turned back and could not follow Jesus. Furthermore, who would leave the very land of his ancestors?

People find themselves caught in a similar dilemma from time to time. Some good persons, nice persons, are property owners above all else. The Bible says nothing against the ownership of property as such, but it has a great deal to say about the conflicts and desires that evidence themselves within those who live for their property and those who live for God.

Think, for example, of newcomers to a new suburban area where other people have had property for a long time and have always been the persons to make the decisions on the school board, in the township, and in all other ways. The new people moving in are running their businesses in a nearby city. Some are teachers in the high school or are professors at the university; others are in occupations that do not allow them to amass a great deal of property. The settled heads of families say: "Who are these new people that stand up and try to tell us what to do? Let those who have long owned the property and paid the taxes make the decisions."

The merit of the proposals made by new families are not considered. Nor is much attention paid to the advice of new board members whose occupations do not require property. Established citizens find themselves returning again and again to the security valued by the man in the Scriptures: a house, a home, a settled place in life, land they call their own.

There is also the desire for a *place* in community institutions—including the church. It is so easy to identify the kingdom of God with brick, mortar, and stained-glass windows. When I was eight, I attended the church that I later joined. My first Sunday in the Primary department remains unforgettable because green screens of a new kind of cloth that I had never seen before separated one class from another. Sitting there and listening to the lesson, I was fascinated by those screens. Several years ago I returned to that church and eagerly went to the Primary department. How very disappointing! The screens had disappeared—much for the better. Partitions of celotex had been erected. The noise from one squirmy little group no longer traveled to the next one. But all of this disappointed me emotionally because, in some way, I had associated my first memory of Bible study and church with those green screens.

Property, physical equipment, and location have symbolic value. People often associate some kind of church furnishings, or some kind of architecture, or a church building in one place as part of their "religion." For them, God is in a certain place.

Jesus Christ challenged this emphasis upon the security of a physical dwelling place—either for an eternal God or for a man—and placed it upon a continuing, sustaining relationship with him. When a fourth of the United States population moves each year, people must give up the furniture, the buildings, the order of service—all those things which have been so dear. But as they go to another place and worship with a different congregation, they find other persons who are devoted to the same God; although, they may worship him in a different way and in a different kind of building.

Divine call strives with family loyalty also. Jesus called a man who said, "Lord, let me first go and bury my father." For any Jewish son, this was certainly an honorable desire. But Jesus said to him, "Leave the dead to bury their own dead, but as for you, go and proclaim the kingdom of God." How are we going to solve a problem like this? In churches today, most people who made their confession of faith have been in a Sunday School and are from homes where some allegiance to the family exists. Is Jesus calling us to forsake this godly heritage? Is this not speaking against the home, the most natural environment for evangelism, dedication, and Christian nurture? Certainly the family counts, but the question is, how much? It is a mistake for the family to count too much, to believe that the desire to be loved by others in the security of the home must come before anything else. Thereby, we become enslaved to the ways of those who have gone before us. We find ourselves following only those who agree with mother and father and grandmother and grandfather. We find ourselves rejecting those who have anything else to say.

The conflict of family loyalty is great in the area of religious commitment. One man furiously said to a pastor, "My son is not going to join the church because of the things that your church did to my father." That father, not a Christian, had previously had his gambling business ruined by the stand taken by the churches in his town. His son, who worshiped his father, would now keep his own son from joining the church because of what had happened to one whom he loved.

Can commitment to God go beyond family pride when a member of the family is disciplined by Christian principles? Can we bear the anxiety of coming out from under the security of home and neighborhood in order to follow Jesus Christ who said, "I am come to set daughter-in-law against mother-in-law, father-in-law against son-in-law"? Members of the same household may even become enemies of one another for the sake of their commitment to Christ.

We are so accustomed to defending our clan, our class, our race. And, our commitment is so secure in these things that we hardly understand God's call to go beyond this and commit ourselves to other families, other people, other nationalities, and other cultures.

The decision is difficult—so difficult that Jesus warned men in the beginning that they would be fickle in their decisions. The pressures are great, and the man who is not ready to lay aside his inner reserve of self will find shortly that he is falling by the wayside. One man said, "I will follow you Lord, but let me first say farewell to those at my home." But Jesus said to him, "No one who puts his hand to the plow and looks back is fit for the kingdom of God." This kind of commitment includes steadfastness. It means that we must have a sense of integrity, that we are not to be swayed by impulse or by intensity of feeling. But we must weigh thoughtfully the cost of following after Jesus Christ.

Again and again people have been hurt because lip service is strong and pious, but daily practice is weak and hypocritical. In great admiration for an older person we may have thought, Surely one who has prayed, taught, and preached as this person has is the embodiment of Christian ideals. Then we may have gone to this older person in time of crisis and asked for guidance or help, only to receive advice that is pagan and selfish—all for this world.

What about "commitment" and this older person? If, perhaps, a serious pastor, deacon, or teacher had been asked, "Why did you disappoint this young person who trusted you?" he might say, "Well, I never thought that this would really make a difference." Such a leader thinks he has committed himself because, on one occasion, he joined the church and now serves it on Sunday. He does not let the principles of loyalty get in the way of business or social relations.

If these persons were younger, their inconsistency might be explained as inexperience; for in youth, intensity and impulsiveness often characterize commitment. But when an experienced leader talks one way and acts another, we do not say that he is inexperienced; we say that he lacks integrity, that he knows better. He is a man under responsibility. His decisions make a difference in the lives of many people.

Constancy is more and more emphasized as we mature in discipleship. Mixed motivations make steadfast loyalty difficult. There are more decisions to be made about property, about established position, about a family. More people are affected by our attitudes.

The temptation is to solve the responsibilities of discipleship by compartmentalizing life: "business is business," "politics is politics," "what I do in my family is my own concern." Everyone yearns for some privacy, but isolation, either personal or religious, is not a part of discipleship. It is well to remember the rebuke of Jesus: "Why do you call me 'Lord, Lord,' and not do what I tell you?" (Luke 6:46).

It may take a crisis to cause men to act on their convictions as disciples of Christ, Lord of all life. Then politics, business, and property can all be used to serve the kingdom. The crisis might be one such as desegregation. In McComb, Mississippi, there had been bombings and racial disturbances. Only four white leaders of the community opposed the handful of terrorists and militant segregationists who intimidated white and Negro alike. But these four worked until 650 citizens had signed a "Statement of Principles" that there should be equal treatment under the law for all citizens, regardless of race, creed, position, or wealth.

It was a statement that transformed McComb. Public facilities were desegregated, and the bombers were arrested and placed under suspended sentence. But for thoughtful people, the most important result was a feeling that law and order had prevailed because someone had been willing to risk his reputation—perhaps even his business—for what was right.[4] A few had been steadfast while much was at stake. Their constancy gave courage to others.

Surrender—the Beginning of Discipleship.

Discipleship expresses itself in many ways, and to identify it with one social issue, one way of life, or one opportunity for service would be folly. Discipleship is continuous and varied. No disciple can settle down in the belief that he always knows what is expected. There will be new crises and different ways of interpreting Christian principles. In the midst of changing circumstances, no one act or attitude can guarantee faithfulness and righteousness.

Soren Kierkegaard has said that purity of heart is to will *one* thing. For the believer, that one thing is the surrender of his will to the Spirit of Christ. This surrender is not a once-for-all accomplishment. It begins with conversion but continues through a lifetime of learning.

God does not call us because we are pure. He does not call us because we know all we need to know about him. God calls us to begin, to take a great leap into faith. To follow Christ, to "learn of him"—this is the commitment of discipleship.

3

An Enlightened Mind

Many people spend their time habitually seeing only what is apparent. The richness and beauty that could fill their lives and increase their great potential are lost in the narrow furrows of limited understanding.

W. Somerset Maugham writes in *Quartet* about an English country gentleman whose son had just returned home from college. The father was completely engrossed in judging stock shows, in the management of conservative political affairs, and all the routine life of a gentleman farmer. He expected his son to think in terms of business or politics. After dinner one evening, with all the family listening, he raised the momentous question with his son: "Well, my boy, what do you want to do?"

"Father, I should like to play the piano."

"Why, of course, son, you can play the piano whenever you want to," the bewildered father said.

The boy replied that he was not interested in playing the piano one time, he wanted to play the piano as his vocation. The father was struck dumb. He could not imagine a man in his household who would devote all his time to one artistic expression. Like the country gentleman, we, too, are prone to see only what fits into our established pattern of thinking, our self-interests.

Although Jesus' words were truth itself, he did not expect everyone to hear and obey. He knew that the ears of many were "fat," that their eyes were "heavy." Only those who had "ears to hear" would hear. Even the disciples who had spent so much time with him failed to understand all he taught while he walked among them. (Much of Matthew's Gospel shows how Jesus taught his followers about himself.)

But Jesus had taught well. His truth had penetrated the understanding of many of the disciples to the extent that, after his resurrection, they vividly recalled things he had said: "When therefore he was raised from the dead, his disciples remembered that he had said this; and they believed the scripture and the word which Jesus had spoken" (John 2:22). So often they had missed the clear meaning of his teaching. He had said that in three days he would raise up "this temple" when destroyed. At the time, the disciples saw only the physical Temple of Jerusalem where the debate took place. After the resurrection as the light of understanding dawned, they comprehended the deeper significance: "He spoke of the temple of his body" (v. 21).

Jesus knew that it was not enough to speak fine phrases. He dramatized truth, made it relevant. People heard it expressed in terms of their daily experiences. Recalling later, they better understood what Jesus had come to tell them. Jesus knew men's preoccupations, their limitations in learning, their natural inability to understand the full meaning of God's revelation. So, he taught in ways that captured their attention, made them ask questions, made them think. He fastened thought to truth. Thus were the minds of men enlightened.

New Teachings and Methods

Jesus revealed new insights into human nature, understanding of human needs, and God's power in human life. These things the disciples learned as Jesus taught them by parables, miracles, and by active participation in his work.

Parables.—Jesus taught in parables in order to reveal subtle truth that was not readily perceived by the closed minds of insensitive people. His stories are like windows in heaven through which the light of divine truth shines upon life.

Jesus used this method so often that on one occasion the disciples asked him, "Why do you speak to them in parables?" Jesus answered, "To you it has been given to know the secrets of the kingdom of heaven, but to them it has not been given. . . . This is why I speak to them in parables, because seeing they do not see, and hearing they do not hear, nor do they understand" (Matt. 13: 10–13).

Often a story will enlighten the minds of people—especially children—to see significance in life around them that otherwise remains unnoticed.

Mary Poppins came into a household where the father was completely absorbed in the banking business. As a nurse for the children, Mary Poppins told many stories including one about the old woman who sold crumbs at St. Paul's Cathedral so that passersby could feed the birds. The children were fascinated by this story in which the love of people enabled birds to fly up toward heaven and meet the angels of God descending.

On an unusual morning the father decided to take his children to see his bank, and they walked by St. Paul's Cathedral.

"Father, do you see the old woman?" the children asked. The father glanced in her direction.

"Of course, I see her. Come on."

But he really did not see her, for he did not understand the significance of what she was doing. He would not stop and allow his children to spend any of their money for bread crumbs to feed the birds. The hurry and bustle of commerce had consumed his imagination.

Napoleon once said, "Men of imagination rule the world." Jesus captured the imagination of men with parables that revealed eternal truth in the ordinary situations and relationships of daily life.

Unless we see the relevance of Jesus' teachings, to our own growth and maturity, we may remain as inadequate as a woman who tried to explain to her husband the reasons for the long illness of her brother. The husband could not understand the man's illness, for he thought the brother was a good man who should not be suffering as he was. The wife said, "Dear, I remember back in Sunday School that I learned of God as one who punishes us because he loves us. Since my brother was a good man, God is chastising him." The husband grunted and said he could never accept such stuff as that.

The woman's religion was irrelevant because it was still at the level of the oversimplified, black-and-white attitudes of her childhood. She needed to be taught in parables! That is, she needed new insights that would convey truth and would appeal to a materialistic, matter-of-fact husband in an adult world.

What helpful explanations do we have for the confused and perplexing affairs of our lives? How do we relate evil, sickness, and tragedy to the eternal purposes of God? The Christian of enlightened mind seeks by disciplined study, prayer, and conversation to understand the relationship between the events that make up daily living and God's eternal purposes that give meaning to life.

Miracles.—The power of God was incarnate in his Son. His very being was a demonstration of that power. Jesus used it for the spiritual and physical well-being of some men and to convince others who doubted him. After John was thrown into prison, he sent his disciples to ask Jesus if he were indeed the Christ. Jesus' answer was: "Go and tell John what you hear and see: the blind receive their sight and the lame walk, lepers are cleansed and the deaf hear, and the dead are raised up, and the poor have good news preached to them" (Matt. 11:4–5).

We live in a day when the miraculous can scarcely be distinguished from human accomplishment. We are uncertain of the nature of what we see and hear. Some people long for specific and concrete evidence of God's distinctive power in miracles of healing and change. And the sympathetic words of Jesus often come as reassurance to them: "Blessed are those who have not seen and yet believe" (John 20:29).

However, no longing to discern the miraculous in physical healing is greater that the need to see examples of the miracle of a new spirit that transforms a person's life. A little boy is impressed when he sees his father, the strongest man he knows in the world, bow his head and yield himself to someone stronger who is called God. Children learn concepts of words like virtue and character from the example of people who portray their meaning in relationships with these little ones who have nothing but love to give in return. Young people yearn for assurance that older persons will be trustworthy, will "swear to their own hurt, and not change." When someone goes the second mile, or stands for what is right at a time of risk, then they begin to understand the impact of God's power upon the life of a person. The supreme miracles performed by Jesus Christ are the transformed men and women, from the disciples of the first century to the men and women of the twentieth, whose lives are the incarnation of God's love.

Participation.—Jesus' words about an enlightened mind were spoken after the return of seventy disciples who had preached and healed in his name. These men returned with joy to say that even demons were subject to them in the name of Christ. Jesus rejoiced with them, for thereby his power and purpose were extended through the disciples to others (Luke 10:21–22).

We learn by doing. A child learns to tie his shoe by imitating a parent who does it with him. Psychologists have found that "achievement motivation" is greatly increased when parents patiently take time to show a child how to perform a new task.

We learn of Christ by participating in his mission. The challenge of service through a church is not for the extension of an organization; it is for the growth of Christian personality. Sometimes men and women devalue their contribution to God's kingdom because they think that certain sacred words, or a particular amount of knowledge, are necessary before they can witness for Christ. They do not realize that their personal concern for others and the wisdom which they have developed over the years attracts others to the Christian faith.

In one school for Christian leaders, an older woman reported on her visit to a young mother who was new in the community. She found the young mother "trapped" at home with young children, unable to get out because her husband was away on business all week. The young woman was depressed and close to tears. The older woman listened sympathetically, then talked kindly about the necessity of sharing her feelings of loneliness with her husband. Later, they made plans for the young woman to come to the church on Sunday where there would be a place for her, her husband, and the children. "But, oh," the older woman said to those in the class, "I failed to answer all her questions or to tell her how God could answer her needs. I just did not know all that I should say." Another woman in the group commented: "Well, it seems to me that you have done the thing that needed to be done most. You have been a mother in God's name to this young woman at a time when she desperately needed the affection and counsel you could offer. What more could you have done?"

How do we know that our minds are renewed and enlightened, that the miracle of being a new creature in Christ has taken place? It is revealed in our willingness to participate in the work Christ came to do, to make God's redemptive love known upon earth through our lives.

New Wisdom

Before Jesus lived upon the earth, the Jewish teachers had emphasized ritual prayer, the study of the Law, visions, and dreams. When Jesus came, he taught men in the most relevant, personal ways to know God and how to obey him. This new teacher often said: "But *I* say to you. . . ." His was an immediate authority, the embodiment of God's will for men. No secondary source was necessary to know God.

Before Jesus came, men approached God through the priests, sacrifices, and rituals. On the cross, Jesus superseded all high priests, all sacrifices, and rituals. Jesus and the Father are one. All the teachings of the prophets, all the words of the Law, were but shadows of the full revelation of God through his son: "In many and various ways God spoke of old to our fathers by the prophets; but in these last days he has spoken to us by a Son, whom he appointed the heir of all things, through whom also he created the world. He reflects the glory of God and bears the very stamp of his nature" (Heb. 1:1–3).

All this was indeed a new wisdom.

A new kind of wisdom also was to be seen in men: "Who is wise and understanding among you? By his good life let him show his works in the meekness of wisdom. . . . The wisdom from above is first pure, then peaceable, gentle, open to reason, full of mercy and good fruits, without uncertainty or insincerity" (James 3:13-17).

Wisdom and understanding are the virtues of maturity. They help us to fulfil the realistic expectations of people who look for a reflection of Christ in our lives, and they help us to keep our faith amid the uncertainties of a complex world.

James's definition of a wise disciple has not been emphasized strongly enough in the religion of recent years. The emphasis has been on feelings, on spontaneous expression of emotion, on immediate impulses: "Come now! Don't wait! You'll understand later." The result is that generations of malformed Christians have grown up. Much energy has been concentrated on a "heartfelt" experience, and the new convert has not been provided with understanding and guidance for good living and thinking. How a person acts and thinks is as important in expressing his Christian faith as how he feels.

After conversations with seventy-three converts in national revival meetings, Dr. Pitirim Sorokin found that half "talked more like fundamentalists," but none showed much change in outward conduct.[5] They had missed the "renewal of the mind" which is so important a part of Christian discipleship.

When Jonathan Edwards was trying to understand the changes that had taken place in the lives of converts after the great awakening of 1740, he concluded that the people had a "new sense of religion." Changes in persons' lives were varied: some were gradual, some were sudden, some were quite apparent, and some were hardly visible. In summarizing what he saw, Mr. Edwards felt that all the converts had "an appreciation of the beauty and moral excellence of things." [6] They saw God, themselves, other people, and the world in a broader and deeper relationship than ever before. That this leader of the first great revival in America should lay great stress upon a "new sense of religion," upon appreciation, upon enjoyment of holy things, is significant.

Jesus gave us a new wisdom about the nature of God and how we are to be related to him. We are to think his very thoughts after him: "Be transformed by the renewal of your mind, that you may prove what is the will of God, what is good and acceptable and perfect" (Rom. 12:2). He has sent the Holy Spirit to dispense this new wisdom, to transform our thinking, to guide us in service and relationships with our fellowmen.

4

Primitive and Prophetic Prayer

The word "wisdom" suggests more than mere common sense, and "wisdom from above" implies a mind enlightened by divine truth—knowledge that comes from God, knowledge that surpasses human thought.

Although Paul had a direct encounter with Jesus Christ and his whole theology was built upon that experience, he relied upon the "mind of the Spirit" to guide him after this confrontation. The relationship was maintained by prayer and meditation. The apostle, who wrote of "renewing the mind," knew the importance of prayer. And, admitting the insufficiency of men in prayer, Paul relied upon the Spirit of God: "The Spirit helps us in our weakness; for we do not know how to pray as we ought, but the Spirit himself intercedes for us (Rom. 8:26).

Magical Prayer

Why do we not pray as we ought? Because certain mistaken ideas of God's power and the use we expect him to make of it in our behalf are mixed with our genuine need and pleas for his help. Our prayers become a mixture of magic and faith.

We distort prayer into magic by believing that God will do whatever we ask him to do. This is the essence of magic. A worshiper, believing that he knows a divinity and the formula for calling on him, thinks that he can get what he wants, since the god cannot be separated from the nature over which he is supposed to rule. In primitive religions, natives guard carefully the name of their god. They protect the ceremonies and the places where they call on him. They believe that if they can call on him in a holy place, he will do as they desire. An Old Testament example was Naaman the Syrian who asked the prophet Elisha for "two mules burden of earth," so he could spread it out in his place of prayer in Damascus. Naaman thought that to kneel on such earth would make his prayer more effective.

Even today, some people still think that their prayers will be heard if they are said in church, or if a holy man, a minister or someone else, prays with them. And there are preachers who proclaim that "if you ask anything in the name of Jesus, he'll have to do it for you."

This kind of prayer is characteristic of nature religions, but it is often spoken by Christians during a time of urgent need. Its purpose is to win God to man's purposes. Along with this kind of prayer often goes a bargain: "Lord, if you will grant this, I will serve you all my days."

Primitive, magical prayer is presented in many best sellers in religion. Louis Schneider and Sanford M. Dornbusch, authors of *Popular Religion,* found that forty-six best sellers from 1875 to 1955 united God's will with man's convenience. One current favorite, Norman Vincent Peale, assured his readers that if they would think money, they would get money. By following ten easy steps of thought control each day, believers would be assured of God's power for their lives.

What is wrong with this kind of prayer? Usually, it is abandoned when the believer doesn't get what he wants. This was revealed in a study in 1950 of mothers who prayed for the recovery of sick children. At the first stage of the children's illness, many mothers prayed. They asked God to heal their children. But when the children became weaker because of incurable diseases, most of their mothers stopped praying. Why talk to God? It didn't do any good, they thought.

But other mothers continued to pray. Why? Because in prayer there was fellowship with God. Although they did not receive what they prayed for, they did receive what they needed—strength through communion with a Heavenly Father who knew their suffering.

If the group of mothers first mentioned had recognized prayer as communion with God, they also might have had his continued fellowship and strength. But for them, prayer was petition—asking for something. When they didn't get the specific thing they wanted, they stopped talking with God.

Belief in magical prayer reflects a Christian's failure to understand his relation to God. It assumes a buddy-buddy relationship. We get God to help us, then we help him. (Does God need our help?) It also assumes that we know what is best for us. God must do as we desire, or we'll desert him.

Prophetic Prayer

The biblical view of prayer is of far greater significance. It begins with a recognition that man does have many needs and that he should make them known to God. The prophets, like Jeremiah, wept before God in frustration. They admitted their need to tell God about all their needs and desires. None of them were rebuked for openly expressing their feelings to God.

In the prayers of the prophets, there was no pride, no telling God what he must do. Instead, they recognized God's holiness and man's limitations. Abraham pled for the righteous of Sodom, but admitted before God that he was but "dust and ashes." Who was he to ask anything of Jehovah?

Knowledge of the distinction between infinite God and finite man is a mark of prophetic prayer. God is holy and righteous. We come to him acknowledging our need, admitting our insufficient strength and our cloudy judgment. The worshiper calls upon God for direction and guidance according to his holy purposes. Human desire is expressed, but it is to be molded by the divine will.

Prophetic prayer expresses the entire range of human feelings. But each person needs fellowship with God above all other things. Prayer at its best is a living communion between persons and God. God is separated from us in holiness and power, but he is personal and is present with us in the Holy Spirit.

Prayer of Commitment

Because the Lord was present with the disciples, they could learn about prayer by watching him pray.

Still, they could not understand all that happened when their master talked to the Heavenly Father. So it was natural for them to ask, after he had been in prayer, "Lord, teach us to pray." Jesus prayed what has come to be known as the Lord's Prayer. To call it "the Disciple's Prayer" or "the Model Prayer" would be more accurate.

Almost, Jesus began this prayer with a petition for the coming of God's kingdom. This desire evidently is to be primary in a disciple's commitment. The prayer recognizes the human needs of disciples: "Give us this day our daily bread." Holy commitment and human petition are reconciled by placing the desire for God's kingdom first and depending upon him to fulfil our needs. Instead of pleading for immediate needs to be met—regardless of their urgency, a humble desire to serve God and his kingdom first is expressed.

In the Model Prayer there is a bargain, but it is in the form of a petition that recognizes that God forgives us as we forgive our brethren. It is man who is to meet the conditions, not God. God does not pledge himself to man; rather, man pledges himself to God. We do not bargain for the Father to do something before we begin to serve him.

We forgive in the belief that God will surely forgive us. Forgiveness places much responsibility upon us. We must be willing to accept the consequences of what we ask for. If we wish forgiveness, we should know that we must forgive others. If not, we are like the unforgiving servant. That servant was freely forgiven a large debt by his master. Should he not be merciful to those who owed him a small debt? In that parable Jesus shed light upon the meaning of forgiveness in the Model Prayer. If we recognize the magnitude of our trespasses that God has cancelled out, we will more freely forgive the trespasses of others against us.

The Model Prayer is not a bargain; it is a recognition of obligation: disciples who are grateful for all that God has done for them should be motivated to show grace to others. Otherwise, they cannot know the fulness of God's mercy.

Who can meet this requirement? All of us fall short of God's glory at this point. We can hardly imagine forgiving our brother seven times. How could we do it seventy times? The rest of the Disciples' Prayer shows Jesus' understanding of our limitations: "Lead us not into temptation, but deliver us from evil." We need deliverance from people who can hurt us; for if they wound us too deeply, forgiveness is extremely difficult. The temptation to hate after being deeply hurt may be more than we can conquer.

The Model Prayer recognizes the limitations of the disciples. Although we are to pray first for God's kingdom and are to be committed to it, Jesus understands that there is a limit to our commitment. We must plead for deliverance from evil and ask that, even in loyalty, we may not be led beyond what we can bear.

Sharing in the Spirit

How may a disciple know how far to go, and in what direction? Jesus promised the Holy Spirit who would be our comforter and instructor in all things.

The book of Acts records many instances of the force with which the Holy Spirit did come upon those who believed. After Pentecost the disciples did not pray further for the Spirit to come upon them; they were already living in the Spirit. Rather, they prayed for a more complete measure of grace, or for specific guidance in the name of the Lord Jesus (Acts 3:1,6; 4:24-30).

For us, this means that the Christian's prayer should be for *more* guidance. We should not begin our devotions as though we knew nothing at all of God's will for our lives. The Spirit is not promised as a sudden illumination in the darkness, but as a counselor who will gradually unfold God's plan, even as he revealed it to our Lord. Jesus moved step by step toward Calvary. Even in the garden of Gethsemane there was no sudden insight, only the ultimate yielding of his will and the realization that he could trust the Father through the suffering he could already foresee.

Some devout persons err in thinking that the answer to prayer will be like the coming of the Spirit at Pentecost. They wait for some complete answer, some soul-shaking experience. More probably, God is already providing the answer to their petitions in the events taking place around them. All of us need some illumination of vision to read the "signs of the times." On other occasions, the answer to our problem may come one step at a time; but we need perspective to interpret what is happening. There are few occasions when a definite vision occurs, like the man telling Paul to come over to Macedonia. More often, we will be like Paul and Barnabas arguing about John Mark, or Paul and James in conflict about the ancient equivalent of racial segregation in the church (Acts 15). Good men on both sides must ask for God's guidance, and no one can say that he has received the entire answer overnight. Even though Peter received a vision, he was led through trial and uncertainty to a final realization that all men were to be accepted into the church on confession of faith alone.

With so much uncertainty about God's answer to their inquiries, how did the early disciples decide what to do? It was through fellowship with one another and guidance from the Holy Spirit. In communion, they learned God's will for their lives.

How was this sharing in the Spirit done among the first Christians? Usually it was in daily worship after eating with fellow Christians in one home. The names of some of the hosts are given: Gaius, Aquila and Priscilla, Nympha (Rom. 16:23; 1 Cor. 16:19; Col. 4:15). Usually these were independent persons, "God fearers," who had broken with the prevailing Gentile religion of their region. They must have possessed courage to do this. Some of them must have been persons of wealth, since a home of considerable size would be necessary for many persons in a city to gather for preaching and fellowship while eating.

Central to the worship service in these home churches was the "daily breaking of the bread" (Acts 2:46). This was a meal which included a prayer of blessing to God and thanks for the bread and wine. Guests contributed food to the meal (1 Cor. 11:21; Acts 20:7–11). This may have been an adaptation of home ritual in Judaism where bread and wine were blessed by the father of the home.

What should this teach us today? The new covenant emphasis seems to be more upon fellowship and guidance through a church or community than through one family. There is no clear statement in the New Testament about a "family altar." This later practice came out of our Puritan heritage in England. Under persecution by the state church, "Independents" had to meet by families for worship. They had no other security. So, great reliance was placed upon daily Bible reading and prayer in the home. When Independents fled to New England, they brought this tradition to the new land. It was further reinforced on the frontier by the scattered population. People *had* to worship as families, for they could seldom meet as a church, and they might not see a minister for months at a time.

Today, family worship is not necessitated by persecution or distance from a church; it has become an expression of common devotion to Christ in which each member gains strength from the faith of all.

Family worship should not be emphasized above community worship in the church. The bond of Christian faith is not the natural organization of the family, but the Holy Spirit which binds people together by their confession of Christ as Lord and Saviour. Christian allegiance may even divide a household, as Jesus foretold in Matthew 10. Or a son may go beyond the vision of his mother and brothers, as Jesus did. His family tried to interrupt his ministry by calling him to come home. Jesus' family thought he was mad!

Protestant religion appeals to individuals, not families. Gerhard E. Lenski,[7] in his study of religion in Detroit, found this to be true. Protestants joined churches as individuals; they had friends in and out of the church; they were members of both church and civic organizations.

In contrast, Detroit Catholics thought of the church in terms of the family. Church attendance was a family affair. So was social life. Catholics got together as families. They made fewer friends at work or outside the home than Protestants did.

Whether group worship is in the home, the church, or a community center, one primary purpose should be the recognition of human frailty. The experience of sharing prayer, Bible study, discussion, and meditation can minister to our natural frailty.

Fellowship in praise of God strengthens the individual personally, disciplines his life, gives guidance for a wider understanding of Christian faith than his individual preoccupations allow.

How is this done? One way is to organize small groups for Bible study, and/or for discussion of moral or theological questions. This does not mean the usual prescribed study course by subjects in printed lessons. The purpose is not to emphasize content and what is already known. Instead, the group selects some book of the Bible; several verses are read; then individuals are asked to comment. Or, questions can be handed in by group members for discussion from week to week. The value of such a meeting was expressed by one person who said: "I've been a church member for years, but I never have been in a class where we could ask *our* questions without being embarrassed. I feel free to do that here."

As people feel free to ask questions, they begin to express their own needs. In one group, a man asked how to gain confidence in himself after he had been suddenly dismissed from his job. He also wondered how he could be Christian enough to overcome resentment.

"Why," said one man, "just look in the mirror every morning and say, 'I'll make good contacts, good sales today.' That's what I do."

"No," the first man said, shaking his head, "that's unrealistic for me. You haven't faced what I have."

Several women expressed sympathy for the depressed man, and one asked if his wife understood what he was going through. The man replied that his wife and children gave him confidence to keep going, but still there was resentment.

Few final solutions result from such discussions, but much fellowship does. There are several limitations for such groups which should be noted:

They are temporary. People usually have no need to explain themselves or explore their basic needs for years and years. The most satisfying groups may exist for several months, or a year, then break up so members can return to other church groups.

They are informal. This is not formal group therapy in which people tell their deepest longings and darkest secrets. There are no controls in such a church group. People can learn a great deal from listening to one another and seeing how others relate to them, but they should not express the violent emotions or irrational opinions that are encouraged in group therapy. A distinction must be made between a voluntary band of relatively healthy indviduals and a collection of neurotics or psychotics who must penetrate the depths of their twisted emotions before they can be healed.

They need secure leadership. Usually, enough mature people are in a church of five hundred people to keep an unstructured group on an even keel. But sometimes, a leader feels that he must give all the answers; he can't stay on the sidelines when someone else is getting attention. Or, a leader may be fascinated with everyone's problems and try to extract all the pathological symptoms he can from group members. Then, there is the leader who doesn't lead at all; he just sits and says "hmm." A more secure leader will offer an interpretation when the group is stuck, or encourage someone who has made his first, tentative declaration, or stay with a difficult but important question when some people become anxious and try to change the subject. Some suggestion for group leaders may be found in *Dynamic Christian Leadership,* published by the American Baptist Publication Society, Philadelphia, Pennsylvania.

Christian fellowship can encourage and nourish spiritual growth. This kind of group is sometimes referred to as being "task oriented." Its purpose is to help one another—sustaining the weak, comforting the afflicted, challenging the complacent, witnessing to the lost.

Paul reminded the Corinthian church that they had become too self-centered and wild in their religious expression (1 Cor. 14:13-19). How would an unbeliever be convicted by the undisciplined ravings of those who "spoke in tongues"? Five sober words from the soul would have more impact than ten thousand assorted sounds that no one understood.

Paul called for prophets, wise men to interpret what was going on, to clarify the confusion, and to discipline those whose communication was disorganized. That people have feelings that they need to express before God and other people must be recognized. In fact, one reason that people worship in "tongues" is that they lack opportunity for emotional expression in established churches. "All bottled up," such individuals find sudden relief in babbling incoherently.

But, they do not take responsibility for what they say. The willingness to be understood so that others may know us as we are and judge us in the light of our pronouncements is a criteria of prophetic worship.

Paul believed in prayer with emotion. But, he writes: "I will pray with the spirit and I will pray with the mind also" (v. 15). He will bring an enlightened mind to his worship experience.

5

A New Kind of Piety

Worship through prayer and shared experience helps us to know God's way for our lives. Also, by intelligent reflection and dedicated action, his will is revealed. To these must be added some formal religious behavior, some habits of devotion. But, why would this be necessary if people live "by the Spirit," in freedom from the Law of which Paul writes?

Ritual is necessary because we are imperfect people. We cannot remember to do spontaneously all the things that are important to our lives. So, we imbed them in a daily or weekly routine and special seasonal religious observances—Christmas, Easter. Almost every significant function of life is part of a ritual. Religion is an essential part of life. Therefore, it needs to have some expression in habits, repetitive behavior, holidays and special occasions. The observance of these religious habits is often called "piety."

Jesus' practices were examples of piety in the best sense of the word. He gave thanks before meals, and it was his custom to attend the synagogue and Temple worship, although the passages do not say that he worshiped while he was in the Temple.[8] He spent nights in prayer and also prayed openly.[9]

Much of Jesus' ministry was spent answering questions about piety—getting in and out of conflicts with religious people over the observance of customs pertaining to the sabbath, the Temple, or prayer. Why did he give so much attention to these things? Why did he not dismiss them and say that, since he fulfilled the Law, his disciples should not be bothered with such matters any more?

Our Lord attached importance to ritual because he knew the frailty of men. We need specific, routine ways to remind us of God and of our obligations to him. We are not, like Jesus, so constantly close to God that we spontaneously turn to him as our Father. We need reminders and definite channels for expression of our religious devotion.

Imperfect men develop religious institutions in order to perpetuate the first, intimate sense of God's presence. *If* Jesus had remained on earth, he might not have founded a new community, the church. He certainly developed no organization for it while he was here. But when he ascended, the organization began to develop because men have natural needs for a time, a place, and the habit of worship.

Much criticism has been aimed at "institutional Christianity" and "religionless Christianity" in the last half of the twentieth century. But how could faith endure among faithless men without some habits by which

Christians could recall and express the Spirit that empowers them? What permanence would Christianity have if it were dependent only upon spontaneous outpourings like the once-known day of Pentecost?

The problem arises not over piety as such, or with institutions, or religious habits, but because of our overdependence upon them. We have identified Christian character with religious practice, or have thought that the church building or organization must be preserved, even if some vital witness for Christ is silenced. In every generation there are ministers and dedicated laymen who are dismissed or disciplined by a complacent congregation or denomination for "disturbing the peace of Zion." It might be Roger Williams denouncing the state religion in New England, or John Fee protesting slavery in Kentucky, or a hundred ministers a year removed from southern pulpits for supporting racial desegregation in the 1950's. In one section of the country a man is silenced for speaking against gambling, in another for showing the evils of social drinking. On each occasion the rationale is: "We must not split our church," or "We must keep our denomination together—keep out these divisive issues."

Dead Devotion

Jesus' conflict was not with piety as such, but with piety that was not empowered by a spirit of love. He had to fight a dead devotionalism that shows up in the same forms even today.

Many times our Lord met the problem of petty scrupulosity. The Pharisees protested that he did not wash before dinner. Jesus rebuked them, saying that they paid so much attention to the outside of the cup (the self) that they did not notice the corrosion (extortion and wickedness) on the inside (Luke 11:37–41). Or some religious leaders were alarmed that the disciples "worked" on the sabbath—they plucked and ate ears of grain as they walked through a grainfield. Jesus replied: "The Son of man is lord of the sabbath" (Luke 6:5).

The deadness of this legalism was seen in the failure of these objectors to be concerned with doing good on the sabbath. Jesus healed a man with a withered hand and said: "I ask you, is it lawful on the sabbath to do good or to do harm, to save life or to destroy it?" (Luke 6:9). The legalists did not answer; they were bound up in their rules. But they were filled with fury that he should have exposed their unconcern for people in distress, that he had questioned their "religion."

Ritual without love is a mournful business. Jesus noted the hypocrites who looked terrible after fasting. He advised his disciples to wash their faces, to look well, and to let no one know that they were doing without food for a godly purpose.

Legalism is self-deception as well as an attempt to deceive others. Jesus noted that those who "hold fast the tradition of men" would find a legal loophole to prevent them from supporting their parents. Their pretense of obedience to God through a tradition actually made void his word (Mark 7:13).

The self-concern of the legalist is observed in his willingness to make an exception of himself, whether by escaping financial responsibility for the family, or by protecting his social and economic interests when church and society are challenged to change. Such a person was a prominent landowner whose self-interest showed through his legalism. The landowner of about one thousand acres believed in tithing. "For," he said, "if I don't give back part to the Lord, he'll take away all I have." Whenever a prize bull or milk cow became ill, the owner would say: "It's time for me to up my tithe. The Lord is reminding me!" This man always paid by check, and he gave it only two or three times a year—when he had a crisis like the sick cow. Since he was an usher, he would put his check in the plate, face up, before he passed the plate down the first aisle. That gesture, plus the spurt in the offering for that week, announced to all the magnificance of his gift.

Whenever there was a special need for money, the landowner decided whether it should be taken. Everyone knew he would give the largest amount. After an associational meeting, several deacons came back to the church proposing an annual budget. The landowner fought it saying, "The Bible don't say nothing about a budget." The proposal was delayed for three years, while people said: "Mr. —— doesn't want a budget because then the *people* will decide what's to be spent each year. He wants to make all the decisions himself."

What is the answer to religious legalism? How can we be regular in our religious practices without judging others on the same basis? How can we keep pride out of our careful observance of good conduct?

Jesus' answers seem to imply that voluntary religious service and inner holiness are to be in harmony. The dangers of legalism are then avoided in two ways.

Voluntary religious service eliminates the compulsive element in legalism. The landowner felt that he *must* tithe, or the Lord would take away all he had. There was nothing voluntary in his giving. In pride and fear he placed his check face up in the plate.

But the biblical teaching is: God loves a *cheerful* giver. The noblest impulse for religious action is the knowledge that God loves us. As John says, "We love because he first loved us." He gave himself for us, so we give ourselves in service to him.

The service is voluntary.

Unconscious Piety

This motive of love is not to be restricted through specific, legal channels. The command is general. Jesus did not say that we must read the Bible daily, come to church twice on Sunday, and give a tenth of our income to show our love. To do these things is right; but the great concern of our Lord was that men act appropriately whenever it was necessary to serve the needs of others. So, he healed men on the sabbath while the legalists stood by and criticized him.

Voluntary religious service depends not only upon Jesus' example, but also upon our own background and experience. A person who has been taught basic reasons for good conduct, can usually decide what is right on the basis of what he sees is involved at the moment. He applies learned basic principles to specific situations. Psychologists call this a "rational conscience."

Parental training is most important. A child learns as his parents explain the reasons for rules or instructions and praise or blame him for his application and understanding of them. For example, an eight-year-old was told to stay in the house, to let no one in, and to let the dog out of his pen for protection while the mother went across the street to take some food to a sick neighbor. When the mother returned, she found that the dog was in the pen and the daughter was in the yard.

"What did I tell you to do!" said the irate mother. "Mommy," replied the child, "I know you told me to stay in the house and let out the dog. But Jimmy (a six-year-old neighbor) came by to bring us our shovel. He's scared of Duffy (the dog) and was out in the yard yelling. So I put Duffy in his pen. Then I stood here in the yard to see if he got down the street before I let Duffy out again."

That was the dawning of a rational conscience. Fortunately for its development, the mother praised her child for thinking of what was right for another child even though temporary instructions were disobeyed.

Most of us have a mixture of the rational conscience with another kind, the "infantile conscience." The latter results from a rigid application of set standards by unimaginative parents. Any deviation from "thou shalt not" is punished, no matter how sensible the exception may be. Also, fear that God stands behind the parent and will add his disapproval to that of the parent is instilled in the child. The legalistic landowner grew up thinking that

God would punish him if he didn't give a tithe, perhaps because he had been taught that his parents would punish him if he didn't do just as they said.

Because of this mixture, legalism often remains in the background of voluntary religious action even for mature Christians. Memory-traces from the past continue to influence us, even though we are far from the home-town, the childhood pastor, parents, or friends. One alert young wife, whose husband had been transferred from the deep South to a mid-western city, was always restless on Sunday evening. The church which they loyally supported had a Sunday morning worship service and several other meetings during the week. The wife was happy in her church work, but she said to her husband: "I just don't feel easy about sitting at home on Sunday night. I feel like I'm missing something." "You are," he said. "You've always gone to Sunday evening young people's meetings, church, and usually a party in some church member's home afterwards. Sunday evening was a big social affair for your crowd down South." "Oh no!" replied the wife, "it was a *religious* duty." "Well," said the husband, "it never looked like that to me—you had too much fun."

What was the young woman saying? Habit, religion, and social life were all bound up in Sunday evening activities. She could not separate one from the other. She felt vaguely guilty about the loss of a religious ritual—Sunday preaching after dark. Her husband saw another part of her problem—the lack of social life at an expected time in the week. He will have to be sympathetic with the fact that his wife is still bound by some legalistic patterns. She feels that God should be worshiped at a particular hour of the week. Or, as one country lady said: "On Sunday I just feel it's *right* to come to church after dark."

Many good purposes have been served by Sunday evening young people's meetings, church services, and parties in a home. So long as the primary purposes remain, these rituals have religious meaning. Sometimes, the pious habit has good motivation, as in the case of the young wife. She enjoyed good preaching and the society of Christian people.

In other instances the motivation is not so healthy. Jesus rebuked the legalists of his day, not only for perpetuating rituals that had no more meaning, but also for using those rituals for reasons of pride and self-esteem. They often covered their impious actions with pious forms or phrases.

Inner holiness, in harmony with the voluntary religious service, also helps to avoid the danger of legalism. Jesus taught that a man should leave his gift before the altar of God, go to his brother and be reconciled, then come and offer his tithe. In this he was in agreement with the prophets before him who had called on religious people to rend their hearts and not their garments, to let justice flow down like a mighty stream. They knew that the Lord was not pleased with the offering of a thousand cattle, so long as widows and orphans were oppressed, and justice was reserved for the rich and powerful.

When Jesus presented the principles of inner holiness

in the Sermon on the Mount, the people were astonished at his teaching. He had taught them to look behind the action to the motivation, to consider the character of the person as well as the size of the gift. He praised a widow who gave all she had rather than the rich man who put in many pounds of silver out of his abundance.

What can be said today of this requirement? Who is able to be pure in his motivation? A schoolteacher told of an incident concerning a friend who was a deacon in their church. One Sunday a visiting minister, reading from the Revised Standard Version of the New Testament, quoted the words of Jesus: "I say to you that every one who looks at a woman lustfully has already committed adultery with her in his heart" (Matt. 5:28). The application was so forceful that the perturbed deacon ran into his schoolteacher friend as they left the church.

"Watch out, Brake," said the deacon.

"Why the hurry?"

"Well," he answered, "I got to get home and look in my Bible. If it says the same as that preacher read, I'm a goner!"

If judged by the requirement of a pure imagination, every man and woman is a "goner." Their only hope is in a steadfast desire to love God. We call this singleness of purpose "purity of heart." The desire, the intention is to do good, to show love for neighbor. But, in humility, we must recognize that most pious thoughts are a mixture of godly intent and personal desire. The treasure of God's spirit is in an earthen vessel. The work of purification goes on, but no perfection is attained.

The recognition of mixed motivation helps us to defeat spiritual pride. We hope that our godly intentions and actions will be well received by God and man, but we had better not boast about them. If a man has any occasion to boast, then let him, like Paul, glory in the Lord alone.

Godly piety does not prompt a man to boast because it is unconscious. In humility and contrition, the disciple counts his actions as less than those of all his brethren. Why should he be praised for doing what any Christian should do? What has he done? He has absorbed the meaning of discipleship so thoroughly that he attaches no special significance to acts of love or sacrifice. For such a person to be called "loving" or "holy" would make him extremely uncomfortable. He is so aware of both good and evil within him and knows himself so well that he laughs at any pretension of sainthood.

To accept the loving actions of these unconscious saints is certainly easier than to listen to the "holier-than-thou" ones. The latter irritate people with their self-conscious piety. We are suspicious of them. If they *really* are servants of a Holy God, why do they act so holy themselves? They are but men. Why do they not identify with the brokenhearted, the conspicuous sinner, the insecure neurotic? Although we may not have endured the tragedy and suffering of some people around us, we can certainly recognize the possibility that calamity could befall us as well. This should prompt us to humbly pray, "Lead us not into temptation!"

The n nselfconscious. It is un-
strained. I

But h the twig is bent, so the
tree will oles, and stakes to keep
young sa an backyards. But when
they are opes rot away and knock
out the ontradictory, but unconscious pi reful attention to regulations an erstanding starts in ritual
as well a A child is taught to obey
certain r nows why they are neces-
sary. We dramatize Thanksgiving, Christmas, Easter to portray spiritual meaning and to remind us of our religious obligations. We lead children to pray a long time before they know the difference between an earthly father and a Heavenly Father.

Rodger D. Eakin

Godly piety grows best in natural surroundings. It is rooted in important routines. Usually children begin praying at mealtime and bedtime. These are the natural times for families to be together and for children and parents to feel close to one another. Love and gratitude to God are appropriately expressed at times when these feelings arise naturally out of human circumstances—the family about a table, a mother or father in a quiet bedroom with the child.

Graciousness toward others is usually a matter of *do's* and *don't's* in early life. Children are taught not to interrupt, to take turns, to share. At first, instruction seems legalistic; but in the years to come, the regulations will have sunk into the subconscious, and consideration of others will seem completely natural.

There is no straight line between the teaching of regulations in childhood and the unconscious observance of piety in adulthood. The "traditions of men" must be flexible. The rules and regulations of the elders are to be broken and cast aside and are to be replaced by voluntary action, as a person matures.

This may sound very disturbing to inflexible persons suffering from "infantile conscience." Their philosophy is expressed in comments such as: "Oh, if you don't make a young person go to church every Sunday, then what will happen to his religion?" They think that one exception will cause the collapse of all moral and religious training. The piety taught since childhood would not disintegrate that rapidly—unless it was built on a loveless legalism. In that case, the young person may drop religious observances as soon as he is old enough to defy his family. But if the ritual has been developed in loving relationships, it is not likely to disappear. It will endure into adulthood in another city, another state, another church—as the example of the young wife has shown.

The most natural solution is to change expression of the habit according to the growth of the individual. A junior-age child may enjoy daily Bible reading and memorization of the Scriptures. A young person may be more attracted by specific study in depth of a historical period in biblical history, or by a book of the Bible that speaks to a current social or personal problem, or to some philosophical or theological question relevant to the needs of the age. An adolescent may decide that saying prayers every night is "silly," or he may just stop praying and say nothing to his parents. Parents will do better to talk openly about times when prayer has been important in their *adult* lives than to make a young person feel guilty about rejecting a regular practice of childhood as he now takes the first steps of "grown-up" consciousness.

Adults change their religious rituals as the circumstances of life are altered. Young married couples may sleep late and attend a morning church service at eleven o'clock. A few years later perhaps, a little two-legged alarm clock goes off at 6 A.M. on Sunday like any other day. They may go to church for an eight-thirty service, then one will come home with the baby for its morning nap while the other attends Sunday School. For five or ten years, parents of a growing family may be so busy with children that they do little more than attend one church service. In middle age, they may attend many church meetings; then they are able to take more community responsibility. Later, in the loneliness of old age or widowhood, a person may be at the church almost every time the doors are open.

Thus do religious observances change with the responsibilities of life. A whole church schedule may be altered when a culture pattern is changed. Early Methodists in England had their prayer and Bible study on Saturday evening. It was the only time they could get workmen and their families together. But in twentieth-century America, families think Saturday is a family, date, or party night. The time and place for religious observances depends upon the needs of a group of people. One church in a changing community decided to have "church school" three nights in a week in order to achieve more thorough teaching and to attract some people in the neighborhood who didn't want to come on Sunday morning and sit with "dressed-up people" ready for the worship service. A working woman in a print dress could come on Tuesday night to the educational building and feel at ease. She would have felt conspicuous on Sunday morning with women in their "Sunday best."

However, some people do not change in certain attitudes and actions despite circumstances or class. This stability is a basic test of piety. It does not depend on a static culture, group approval, or regulations handed down from childhood. This piety is that of the man who "swears to his own hurt, and does not change." His moral way of life is so much a part of him that it flourishes under unusual and trying conditions, in places where only he sees its significance.

A doctor of "the old school," in conference with a fussy patient, was observed by a medical student. The patient was a loud, demanding woman. It was 6:30 P.M. and the doctor had been in the hospital since 7:30 A.M. Nevertheless, he rose from his desk, bowed slightly to the woman, and asked her to sit down. She disregarded his courtesy and continued to storm out her complaints. The doctor walked from behind the desk, motioned down the hall in the direction of the service that the woman was seeking, and walked with her to her destination. There was no one in the corridor to see the kindness and courtesy of this man. The medical student was in a cubicle across the hall. The doctor felt no need to be seen acting with graciousness. He did not even "see" himself; he was acting without premeditation in accord with the patterns of a lifetime of training.

Mores and Morality

However, to take for granted our adult manners and assume that what is "natural" to us will be godly piety is dangerous. The mores of an age are learned along with the morals of religion. Our culture is changing. Manners that once seemed so reasonable and relevant to the pre-World War II world are often considered archaic today.

The danger lies in our effort to perpetuate the mores, the customs of a culture, along with the morality that transcends any culture. Some distinction must be made between the manners that belong to our age, our region, and the piety that is the ageless inheritance of Christian faith.

The problem of ritual in a transitional society has been described by James H. S. Bossard and Eleanor S. Boll.[10] They noted the movement in the last hundred years from a religious to a secular orientation in morals and society. Families are smaller and more individualized, more child-centered now, whereas they used to be adult-centered. Children are seen *and* heard today. Living in the family is more democratic. Families grow up in urban environments where there is no neighborhood enclosure to see that customs are kept, manners noted, transgressions reported.

Because of these many changes, piety cannot survive on unchanging custom. The rituals of today must symbolize in action the purposes for which a family, a church, a nation will live. New religious habits must be formed by each generation in each changing social system. This is possible when piety is based upon an inner motivation of love and a voluntary service appropriate to the needs of those who require our help. Some of the old ritual forms will remain with us, but the disciple must be ready for the new wine of the gospel to break the old wineskins of fond and established religious custom.

6

Games People Play

New piety in a changing society calls for sound judgment. But sound judgment is often beclouded by self-interest and self-deception. People do not really hear most information accurately; furthermore, they distort it for their own convenience. People see, hear, and use what they want and what will make them comfortable. Then, they discard the rest.

Jesus talked about this problem when he said that his critics were like children who called on others to dance, and they would not. Then they changed the game to wailing, and still there was no response. What was to be done with people who just seemed to be "playing games" with the Messiah? When John the Baptist came eating no bread and drinking no wine, they thought he had a demon. Jesus came eating and drinking, and people accused him of being a friend of sinners and drunkards (Luke 7:31–35).

Self-interest was so strong that it kept people from hearing much that Jesus said. The radical demands of the gospels were filtered out, and the audience heard what they *wanted* to hear. Even when Jesus pronounced direct judgment on the legalists who blindly led the people into empty, unloving ritualism, they could not believe that he was speaking of them. They said, "Are we blind also?" Jesus replied, "If you were not blind, you would not have asked the question."

How blind—or dumb—are we to the requirements of discipleship? How much do we deceive ourselves into thinking that we are playing a religious part that is not real?

In the book *Games People Play*, Eric Berne[11] has described the ways in which people pretend they are different from what they really are. They imagine what kind of person they wish to be, then interpret their thoughts and actions in the light of this mental image. But too often it is a distorted image of the true self—a living caricature.

There is nothing wrong with a child's playacting when the youngster knows what he is doing. In fact, that is one way by which children try out the kind of work, or adult manners, which they later will assume "for real." Dr. Tom Bennett found that many ministers first thought of preaching when, as children, they "played church." Out of that childish imagination, in imitation of an adored adult or ceremony, there grew later the mature response to the call to a church vocation.

Of course, there is a reverse order of such play-acting. The world is a playground where grown-up day-dreamers play games—and they are not dressed for sports! They are dressed handsomely for dinner, a date, a business engagement. They think that their costume makes them a particular kind of person. It is supposed to add dignity to their character or success to their sales story. Does it really? It may attract some attention and tell of their taste, but outward appearance is not enough.

People can play games in at least two ways: they can deceive themselves, or they can deceive others.

Self-deception can end in tragedy. The *Courier-Journal* of September 17, 1965, told the story of "Cecil Padgett: A Hero Fame Seduced, Forgot." Mr. Padgett had been the strong witness for the prosecution in convicting the murderer of Albert Patterson, reform attorney general from Phoenix City, Alabama. For a time after the trial, Padgett was a bodyguard of John Patterson, reform governor of Alabama. Then, a hometown newspaperman said that Padgett "began getting into trouble. I'm sure it was his affinity for publicity. . . . When the thing began to die down and people didn't talk much about him any more, he was kind of like a dope addict—without dope. He took to calling up newspapers as if he were just trying to remind them who he was." Padgett got into more trouble, went West, and died in southern Texas at age thirty-nine. He had been a hero and enjoyed it. But time passed; then there was no audience to applaud him. However, he had continued to play an unnecessary and unrewarding role.

How many heroes have died in bitterness because people would not continue to see them as they had once been seen? And how many would-be heroes are unhappy because no one has ever recognized them for what they think they are?

Talking about "heroes" may give the impression that

only aggressive people deceive themselves. Self-deception can be equally a problem for passive individuals. One pastor fancied himself to be a "strong preacher." No one knew where this fantastic idea originated. He strained to get words out, paused so long between them that people became nervous, and spoke them in a voice so low that few could hear. When he began to notice the empty pews on Sunday morning, he commented to a close friend: "People here can't understand intellectual messages." When his friend reminded him that many in the congregation had college degrees, the pastor countered: "Well, I mean they can't take deep messages, messages that really stir men's souls. They're complacent, weak. Can't stand strong meat."

Many weak and ineffective men have mumbled their inhibited messages with the inner dream that they are adequate, forceful pulpiteers.

Blinded by self-deceptions, we assume a false strength which may make us unaware of our weakness and failure to achieve Christian ideals. One aggressive, adequate minister told a packed congregation of ministers: "I would give up anything for the sake of the gospel. And so would you. You'd dare anything, even die for Christ, I know!" There were "amens" all over the audience. Outside, Negro children played on the sidewalk. Blocks and blocks of lower-class white public housing and Negro private residences ringed the church on three sides. The church dared to do nothing for these people. All it had done was buy up a dozen frame dwellings, tear them down, and pour on asphalt so that more members could drive in from the suburbs and find parking space. Just what was it that the men in that building were willing to die for?

Playing games does not always deceive others; but sometimes it does. Acting out a role is often done to impress others as much as oneself.

Deception of others may begin innocently enough. The little girl in her "Alice blue gown" may pretend that she is belle of the ball when she looks in a shop window. "The world seems to smile all around." That is the wonderful innocence of childhood.

But what if the sweet young thing won't grow up? uses her baby face to get favors? turns on sex appeal at seventeen or twenty-one, then tries to get out of responsibility or blame? A certain talented young lady used to collect all the information she could about her prospective dates from her friends in high school and the neighborhood. Then, on the afternoon of her date, she would try out the mood or role that she thought would suit this young man. When he arrived, she was ready to be just what he wanted. Now she was never "immoral," but boys and girls did not trust her. "You're never sure what she's thinking or why she says what she says," they would explain.

Grown men can be quite cunning in playing games with business clients. A salesman may quickly spot the prejudice of a prospect, and play up to it. He may see how suggestible a person is to a product that offers prestige and say, "That's just what you need," even when he can plainly see that the customer lacks the credit or culture to use what he is about to buy. Salesmen dismiss the ethical implications of such exploitation by saying, "Oh, that's just business," or "How do I know if they can use it or not?" But they gradually build up distrust. People who are betrayed, whose human weakness is used against them, don't come back. So more and more advertising, more and more gimmicks must be offered by this salesman, or store, to bring in new "suckers."

Double-minded Disciples

With so much playacting in the world, what happens to discipleship? It can become a morality play.

In the Middle Ages, a morality play was a drama in which characters represented some great moral problem or ideal. One person played the devil, another an angel. "The Church" spoke through one actor, "The World" through another. All the words, gestures, and costumes were designed to teach a lesson in good and evil.

Morality plays became unpopular when the modern world grew more complicated. Moral lessons could no longer be presented adequately as all good versus all bad. Even McGuffey's *Readers,* the popular textbooks for children in the one-room schools of the nineteenth century, went out of style because the story endings were so pat. Virtue always triumphed, evil always led to tragedy.

Life is too much a mixture of good and evil for morality plays. Jesus told his disciples that tares and wheat grew up together and that the owner could not cut down one without danger of cutting down the other. One day God would separate them, but that would come with the final judgment. In the meantime, we must contend with some weeds in our Garden of Eden, some selfishness and deception in the heart of a disciple, even as he sincerely tries to serve his Master.

But some Christians still see religion like a morality play. One issue is all good. Another is all bad. And manipulative leaders play up to this naïve way of thinking. Speakers will say: "Jesus would have us vote *this* way," or "That proposition is of Satan." How do they know?

The deception is increased by taking the Lord's name in vain. That is, God and Christ are invoked for the sake of party spirit and to make one side look pious. In a debate about religion and a public issue, one man said: "The last speaker did not name the name of *Jesus.* He did not use the name of *God.* How can we vote for a recommendation that does not name the name above all names?" And so on and so on. The speech was calculated to arouse emotion by its pretense that the symbols of religion gave sacredness to one side. Quite possibly, the previous speaker was too reverent to assume that God was blessing his point of view. He may have believed, and realistically, that godly men were on both sides of a complicated question, that the final decision would be a mixture of good and evil, and that, hopefully, it would produce more of the former than the latter.

We play with religious words, and we also act out our religion. Certain manners and particular kinds of clothing are considered "right"—for Sunday, for ministers, for Christians. Some religious groups wear particular "habits," or suits without buttons, to show their identity. Others expect a "preacher suit" to be dark blue or black. In one meeting only two men, a college president and a seminary professor, did not wear these two colors. They both wore sports coats. Sure enough, the rest of the gentlemen were "of the cloth"—ministers in dark suits.

Does this sound extreme? In one deep South town, a local clergyman said: "I don't really object to that Delta Ministry worker for the National Council of Churches talking to colored people. I guess they need him. But I object to him calling himself a minister."

"Why?"

"Well, the way he dresses. He walks through colored town in a sport shirt—no tie, no coat. I even saw him uptown one day with high-top work shoes on. Our people just don't respect a man like that."

When I asked the Delta worker, a Presbyterian clergyman, why he dressed so informally, he said: "Negroes associate white men in suits with the judge, the white minister, the insurance collector, the banker—all who don't really care about them and who often keep them 'in their place.' I dress casually so they will know I represent a different kind of white man. And it works!"

Both the white minister and the Negro day laborer made decisions about a man's ethical outlook on the basis of his clothes. More was involved, of course; but the suit and the shirt were symbols of "white man's religion" or "black man's friend."

Manners also make a difference. We accept those who act as we do and scorn those who are different. The members of a church in New Jersey were shocked into this realization when they invited teen-agers from the Bronx to attend a party given by teen-agers of the church. Fifteen boys in black leather jackets arrived for the party. The social worker who sent them had taken the precaution of obtaining permission from each parent for this visit. One parent had written: "Take him to Jersey and keep him there." During the program, the boys were noisy and inattentive. When refreshments were served, they grabbed five of everything and stuffed what they could in their pockets. The hosts had never seen such behavior before. They said, "How can we possibly think about a mission in the Bronx to people as unappreciative as these are?"

Differences in manners, dress, and morality lead to major problems in Christian witnessing. Church people say they want to serve the delinquents, the underprivileged, the depraved of their community. But when they contact such people, their words and attitudes do not match.

It is difficult to love those who are different, and we withdraw personally from these ill-mannered and smelly persons who may even be dangerous to us. Only words remain about how our Lord loves them and how much we desire to serve them.

This is the double-mindedness of religion that James notes in his letter. When we look in the mirror of our lives, we see that we really do not love our brother as ourselves. We don't even like to be around him! Then straightway we turn from the mirror, forget the reflection, and piously proclaim that we will witness wherever the Lord leads—but not in the Bronx!

How are we to live as disciples with the knowledge that manners, style of living, dress, and conduct make a difference in our thoughts and contacts with others?

Real Religion

James decided that if a man wanted to know "religion that is pure and undefiled," he would do good works and not be contaminated by secular ways of thinking about who has good manners, fine clothes, and so forth. But how is the disciple to possess this real, genuine religion? Jesus offered an answer in the teaching that followed his talk about "playing games" (Luke 7:31–35).

He went to the home of Simon, a Pharisee, and during dinner a sinner cried at his feet. Jesus told his host a pointed story. A creditor forgave two men. One had a large debt, the other a small one. Who loved the creditor more?

"The one, I suppose, to whom he forgave more," said Simon.

Jesus then told Simon that he had given him no water to wash his feet nor towel to dry them. (These were common courtesies of the day.) But the sinful woman had bathed his feet with her tears and dried them with her hair. She was repentant; and her sins, which were many, were freely forgiven.

What does this story have to do with the double-mindedness of disciples? Two things come from it.

Faith is more real in those who repent and are grate-

ful for Christ's forgivenness. Because they know their imperfections, their double-mindedness, their limitations, these disciples acknowledge the Christ who delivers from sin and gives new life. They know the contrast between the anxieties and inadequacies of their former way of life and the new-found confidence that grows through their Christian faith.

Persons who have honestly faced their limitations do not make extravagant claims about their love for others. They are more realistic. When they seek to serve the depraved and deprived, they humbly ask: "Well, just how much can I stand?" or "What can I do that will *really* have an effect?" They promise people only what they actually think they can deliver. And when others see that these people live up to their promises, they are trusted.

Instead of playing some grand lady-bountiful or knight-on-a-white-horse part, a repentant disciple begins with the little love he actually has for the outcast and hopes the Lord will give the increase of his affection.

For example, a young woman went with her Sunday School class to participate in a program in a mental hospital ward. She felt so inadequate. What could she say to these poor people? While serving refreshments, she noted a woman patient who seemed as withdrawn and as inadequate as the young lady thought herself to be. She sat down by the silent patient and commented on a few things, including the weather. The patient said only one sentence: "I don't know about the weather, for no one ever comes to see me to take me for a walk."

Several times during the week the young lady

thought about that remark. Then she called the hospital and asked if she could take the woman for a walk. It was permitted. Each Sunday afternoon during the summer the two walked from the ward to a nearby park and strolled leisurely back to the hospital. Gradually the patient began to talk about herself, her doubts, her loneliness, her guilt. The young lady didn't know how to answer, but she tried to be sympathetic and continued the walks.

Several months after returning to college, the young lady received a letter and a small package from the former patient. She wrote that she was now out of the hospital and making a living selling cosmetics. She sent one of her products to "her dearest friend" to express appreciation for caring at a time when she could not believe the doctor's assurances that anyone cared. After all, the doctors and nurses were *supposed* to care. But it was through a shy young woman who went out of her way in acts of kindness that the patient was returned to normal living.

In discussing this example in a staff conference, a chaplain noted that this young lady, despite all her feelings of inadequacy, had done more for a withdrawn patient than some of the glib talkers, with their smooth manners and superficial concern, had done for other patients. The socially adequate class members could not really share in the feelings of the patients, for they had never felt alone and inadequate.

How may we learn to care for others without having had their experiences? We learn partly by understanding what counts most in our lives. Then we will have a pretty good idea of what we stand for and what risks we would take, or opportunity we would seek, to defend or declare it.

A person's values are revealed by that to which he gives his devotion and allegiance. Had Simon really cared about Jesus, his actions and attention would have revealed it. But he probably had many things on his mind. Perhaps he was distracted by his many guests and other duties as host. (And is it not the same with us?) The sinful woman had only one person on her mind—the Saviour. Her attention was not distracted. She gave herself unreservedly to his needs.

We can sense the difference between people like Simon and the woman, just as Jesus did. One person welcomes us to a meeting with the same grin that greets every other visitor. His words sound so good: "*Glad* to have you here, suh. Tell me your name. Let me welcome you." But he does not introduce us to anyone else, and when we leave, he hardly notices us. Or, he may even shake hands with us again and say, "Good morning. Glad to have you here, suh. Tell me your name. . . ."

Another person greets us, finds out where we are from, and later introduces us to others from the same area. We know that this person is thinking of our needs: to find friends, to know where we are to stay, to get answers to a dozen questions that new people have when they come to a new city or church.

We can forget the grinning greeter who forgets us. We are more irritated by the "fair-weather" friend who promises so much in the beginning, but deserts us when we have alienated one of the powerful men in his circle. My wife may say: "Have you noticed how A— and C— don't sit with us any more?" or, "Why did A— and C— walk away so quickly the other night, like they didn't want Mr. B— to know they were with us?"

Who is double-minded? What are we to think of such people? Are they still disciples of Christ? Yes, they may be. However, they have forgotten not only what they saw "in the mirror" but they are scared to look very often. They talk much of their accomplishments, drop the names of important associates in conversation, and add or drop names to their list of "friends" according to their standing in the community.

These are weak people. Can we forgive them for playing up to us today and dropping us tomorrow? They really mean "nothing personal" by it. In fact, they may like us very much. And, as they say later when we are back in favor, they were just scared to be seen with us for fear it would irritate a powerful person on whom they were dependent. But, they did not mean to hurt us. They just cannot bear the thought of disapproval in the "power structure." Their values are revealed in their frightened search for important people. Since they are so feeble and frightened, is it not better to forgive them, even as Christ has forgiven us? They certainly are not beyond the forgiveness of our Lord. All his apostles ran away. He knew it would happen, and yet he prayed that they would be strengthened. And when Peter was "converted," Christ charged *him* to strengthen the brethren.

Peter had been playing games. He thought he could serve Jesus to the death; but he ran like the rest. The bitter lesson he learned is repeated in the life of many disciples today. But the forgiveness we experience from our Lord is the strength we need to be realistic and steadfast in our service for him after *we* have been "converted."

7

The Problem of Selective Inattention

Some people play games with religion because they are self-deceived. Misjudgments of self and others can be helped by a realistic knowledge of imperfections and by an acceptance of certain values that should be basic in life.

This prescription for the problem of unreal religion may work well for people who really wish to care about others in the name of Christ. But what about the people who do not care for anyone else? They cannot be made lovable by a little reeducation.

"Religious" persons who really do not care about anyone else are the most difficult ones to deal with. These were the people with whom Jesus was angry. On the sabbath day he asked the people in a synagogue if he should do good or harm, save life or kill? Silently they looked at him and at the man who had come for the healing of his withered hand. Jesus "looked around at them with anger, grieved at their hardness of heart," then cured the man who needed his help (Mark 3:1–6).

Later, Jesus spoke the most direct indictments against these persons: "Woe to you, scribes and Pharisees, hypocrites! for you tithe mint and dill and cummin, and have neglected the weighter matters of the law, justice and mercy and faith; these you ought to have done, without neglecting the others" (Matt. 23:23).

Revival, rather than reeducation, is necessary for such people. They are dead men. Outwardly, they appear righteous, but inwardly they are filled with iniquity (Matt. 23:27–28).

We would prefer to leave these people alone, to do what we can without their help. Although these persons may often be in churches, as they were two thousand years ago, the church organization wishes no conflict with them.

Washington Gladden, who battled the political corruption of New York and Chicago, knew what modern Pharisees were like. He wrote a stanza about them in "Oh Master, Let Me Walk with Thee;" and, even to the present time, hymnbook editors will not include this verse in any hymnal.

The usual churchly solution is to speak out on any issue that will not cause conflict. In this way, the wrath of the "Pharisees" is not incurred. An Episcopal study of laymen and ministers revealed that the church could speak strongly in favor of the United Nations, civil rights, and the dangers of Catholic-Protestant marriages. But although people had many opinions about war, labor, and the place of the government in the control of the economy, no specific pronouncements came forth in these areas. The reason usually given for this silence is the need to keep peace in the church.

In the South, there was a ten-year silence after the

1954 Supreme Court decision on desegregation. The "justification" was: "We cannot talk about a divisive issue because it would split our fellowship." Yet in the midst of silence about a vital issue in life, church people continued to think of themselves as being very religious. All the forms of religious behavior and all the "right" religious beliefs were followed. Mint and dill and cummin were tithed, but what about the weighter matters of justice, mercy, and faith?

Inattention and Self-Interest

Several solutions to the problem of selective inattention have been proposed. One is to do away with all religious forms and ritual. The assumption is that these forms distract people from their basic religious beliefs and from concern for others. Remove the dogma, the teaching, the religious institution, and people will really care for one another.

This solution is usually presented by persons who themselves are selectively inattentive to the problem of human sin. They rightly point to the smoke screen of piety, but confuse the symptom with the cause. The cause of Pharisaism is not religious ritual, but a lack of love for God and fellowmen. Religious habits and beliefs are quite necessary for religious growth. But that growth takes place within people who know that they are imperfect. They do not think that perfection is attained automatically by nine years of perfect Sunday School attendance or ten years of no cursing on the golf course.

In Jesus' denunciation of the Pharisees, their self-interest is apparent as the basic problem in selective inattention.

The prelude to Jesus' last conflict with the Pharisees was his cleansing of the temple. Here people were practicing iniquity in the most holy of places. In the stir that ran through the multitude after this dramatic event, Jesus taught three parables.

First, he described the son who verbally rejected his father's request to work but later repented and labored in the vineyard. A second son verbally assented then went his own way.

Jesus applied this parable to those who thought they were religious, heard all that John the Baptist said to them but never repented. They really disregarded his message because they would not think of themselves as sinners.

On the other hand, the tax collectors and harlots knew what kind of people they were. Their response was to repent, and they believed what John told them.

Jesus' second parable was about the tenants who killed the messengers from the householder, including his son. They were so interested in the profits from the winepress and the inheritance of the son that they could not consider the terrible punishment that would come upon them when the householder avenged himself.

The Pharisees got the point of that story and tried to arrest him, but self-interest deterred them. They feared the multitudes so much that they could not openly oppose one who was thought to be a prophet (Matt. 21:28–46).

Finally, Jesus told the story of the king who sent out

invitations for a wedding feast to all who should have come, but they shamed his request. The king then sent out his servants to bring in guests from thoroughfares and city streets. Those who knew their need could come. Those who were preoccupied with their farms, business, or other matters of self-interest were rejected.

In these three parables, religious form, or ritual, was not the basic problem. The difficulty was with people who were so absorbed in their own way of life that they could give no attention to duty, love, or the most attractive of kingly invitations.

Jesus also said something about the perversion of religious form and teaching. Soon after these parables were spoken, Jesus uttered strong warnings against the Pharisees for binding heavy burdens upon the people in the name of religion. He implied that religious practices were not sacred in themselves. Any of them could be misused by Pharisees and misinterpreted by the people. Much of the "religion" of his day was rejected by the Lord.

Justice, Mercy, and Faith

How then were men to know *true* religion? Jesus certainly did not try to destroy religion; rather, he concentrated upon its great abiding qualities—justice, mercy, and faith. He had not come to destroy the law, but to fulfil it, to give it a deeper and richer meaning than had previously been imagined.

In his earliest conflicts with the Pharisees, Jesus had declared God's requirement: "I desire mercy, and not sacrifice" (Matt. 12:7). Instead of self-preoccupation, he insisted on a God-consciousness that transcended narrow concerns.

The cure for selective inattention is repentence and a new kind of religion that concentrates upon love of God and man. How may these be defined? What do they mean in our lives?

Justice combines mercy and faith. We believe that God has provided his good gifts for the use of all men. This is a part of our faith in a loving God of a good creation. We call this "equalitarian justice."

Not many of us seek this kind of justice for others when we have a comfortable position in life and are unaffected by the iniquities under which others labor. Fair housing, minimum wages, migrant labor laws seem so far away from our comfortable ride from a three-bedroom home to a two-window office. Or, if we work with those who come from deplorable living situations, we may say, "Well, any man who wants to can find a job."

But the earnest disciple asks if each man has really had the same opportunities that have been his. Education and housing are a part of this, but much more is needed. What about the basic desire to live an orderly and clean life? Have father and mother been able to help the child to develop initiative and confidence?

Persons who work with underprivileged people soon learn that the greatest needs are psychological. The deprived person lacks some things that others take for granted.

Sometimes inadequate vocabulary is a problem for

the underprivileged child. He comes to a church kindergarten and is told: "Line up along the red line and face right." The child has never been taught colors. He does not know his right from his left side. "Line up" is a new phrase to him. He stands by himself in frustration. He may be yelled at or pushed into line. Very likely, he will go away angry and disappointed. A teacher who does not understand will sigh and say, "He just would not listen." Has she "done justly" to this child?

Justice demands faith that God wishes children to understand the world and to enjoy it. The work of a disciple is to make this possibility a reality for as many as he can.

Justice that includes mercy is called "distributive justice." It is learned by adequate children about the age of ten or twelve. They have already been taught certain rules and the way in which people should play life's game. This is "equalitarian justice". As they develop moral sensitivity, they realize that some children are handicapped and need to have exceptions made to the rule. The handicap may be an obvious physical defect for which allowances are made. Or, it may be economic deprivation. For example, several children saved some of their lunch money and "found" a Little Theater ticket for one of their friends whose father was unemployed. Explaining this to their friends, they said, "We thought it was right for her to have a chance to go, too. She wanted so much to see the play, but she didn't have the money." This was mercy with justice.

Adults call this "making allowances." Equalitarian justice might demand that a child behave well at 9:00 P.M. in a crowded department store, but distributive justice would make allowances for the emotional drain of three hours in a bewildering mob, plus the physical strain of walking after a full day at school. This is the quality of mercy.

Mercy in practice is the ability to forgive in others what has been forgiven in us. We know how tired we have been on occasions, how our enthusiasm has dropped, and fatigue led to irritability. So we feel understanding sympathy for another person.

In mercy, there also must be judgment. We may have had an occasion that justified our dealing more severely with a person than we actually did. Instead, we choose to deal leniently, and to be merciful. This quality of mercy is often forgotten by persons who, having been hurt, say, "Oh, it does not matter." This is not mercy, it is repression. There should be a recognition of the inconvenience, inconsiderateness, or injustice caused by another person. Mercy does not exclude severe judgment and open recognition of distasteful, harmful attitudes or behavior.

But, judgment becomes mercy when it is combined with forgiveness—forgiveness that is based upon gratitude for what God and others have forgiven in us. We usually are more judgmental toward others in whom we have discovered the same faults as exist in ourselves. But if we have been able to resolve our failures through forgiveness, we are in a better position to show mercy to others. Then it is that we know what should really be forgiven.

A young man, just out of trade school, refused to take instructions from anyone on the machine that he was to operate in a shop. In fact, he bragged to experienced workmen around him about his superior knowledge of this machine. Several months later, when he had had more experience, he sat at lunch with an older operator and said, "I guess you fellows got pretty tired of me spouting off my mouth when I first came to work. I was scared to death and had to act like I knew everything." The merciful answer was: "Sure, kid, lots of us were scared the same way when we first came here. Some settle down and make it; others have to go. We could see that you knew how to handle the tools, so we knew that you would be okay." This kind of mercy gives confidence to insecure people.

Faith may be defined as a confident reliance upon God and an enduring belief in the attainability of his purposes through our lives. In the human venture of life, faith gives us the ability to keep hope in justice and mercy, even though we are frustrated by the injustices and unmerciful attitudes of persons around us.

Godly faith stands when human relationships fall. Faith is strengthened by people who are loyal to us, but there come times when interpersonal relationships fail, and only our faith in God can sustain us.

When we have been disappointed in the integrity of a person or the unfair outcome of a situation, our faith *can* wither and be twisted into cynicism or despair. Some men have been betrayed so often in business that they have decided to "get whatever they can." This kind of "hardhearted business" attitude may even infect church business committees. A building committee found that a bulldozer operator, who was a member of a neighboring congregation, had overcharged them for digging the foundation for their educational building. "After that," said the chairman of the building committee, "we really got tough and beat everybody down for the lowest price we could possibly get." They made up for the loss in the rest of the contracts. But, their church acquired a reputation for "sharp dealing" which it is still trying to live down.

To remain gracious and merciful under such conditions is difficult indeed. But, for a disciple, this is the way of justice and love. For, as Jesus said, if we love only those who love us, we are no better than publicans.

To accept frustration in our own family is often most difficult. A child who has been rejected by a parent in early life may not wish to be reconciled to that parent even though, later, the parent may ask forgiveness. If there is no reconciliation, then both parents and child are in danger of losing faith. The child, who has just reasons to feel bitter, may decide to get from the world what he was denied in a home without love. The parent may become bitter and irascible because he has been denied the child whom he sought to love. He is now at the mercy of his own guilt.

When these temptations seem to overwhelm us, the

recognition of imperfection in every disciple can be a source of comfort. We are not required to be tender and loving in all our natural relationships by our own strength, nor can we require others to show these same qualities toward us. These are gifts from God. If we are loved, we can be grateful. If we are not, our lot is not different from that of many other people. The love of friend and of family is important, but this will pass away. Only God's love is "from everlasting to everlasting."

An immature faith *speaks* of the steadfastness of God's love and uses this to condemn unfaithful loved ones or associates. A mature faith *relies* on the steadfastness of God and pleads with him to increase love between neighbors.

Despite our imperfections, we grow to be like that to which we are basically committed. If we trust God to keep faith with us, we shall grow to be more like his Son. We will learn mercy and justice as we surrender ourselves to God's care and ask these things of him. If we stop short of faith and give way to despair and cynicism, our souls will shrivel. Graciousness, which nourishes their growth, is gone.

An immature faith does not seek spiritual treasures because the search would violate self-interest. Justice requires that we consider the needs of others and go out of our way to be of service to them. Mercy requires that we first accept forgiveness in our own lives and then, with gratitude, allow it to operate toward others. Justice, mercy, forgiveness and gratitude are qualities of growth in grace. When self-interest lures us, or faithless men threaten us, we can remember and be assured by the writer of Hebrews: "We are not of those who shrink back and are destroyed, but of those who have faith and keep their souls" (10:39). Our prayer could be expressed in the words of Washington Gladden:

O Master, let me walk with thee
In lowly paths of service free;
Tell me Thy secret; help me bear
The strain of toil, the fret of care.

Help me the slow of heart to move
By some clear, winning work of love;
Teach me the wayward feet to stay,
And guide them in the homeward way.

Teach me thy patience; still with thee
In closer, dearer company,
In work that keeps faith sweet and strong,
In trust that triumphs over wrong.

In hope that sends a shining ray
Far down the future's broadening way;
In peace that only thou canst give,
With thee, O Master, let me live.

O Master, let me walk with thee
Before the taunting Pharisee;
Help me to bear the sting of spite,
The hate of men who hide thy light.

The sore distress of souls sincere
Who cannot read Thy judgments clear,
The dullness of the multitude
Who dimly guess that thou art good.[12]

8

The Discipline of Discipleship

Growth in grace is a continual challenge to the Christian disciple. The growth may be fast or slow, steady or spasmodic. Luther Buller and a group of theological students found this to be true when they interviewed twenty-six men in Bible classes of rural Kentucky Baptist churches. One man described his succession of commitments to God as being like stairsteps. In his understanding and dedication, he had moved up to one level, stayed there for a while, then moved higher. Another man compared his religious experience to a mountain range. During revival meetings, he reached high peaks of religious feeling, then he descended to valleys of indifference for months. Other men said that after a long period of dormant religion, they had been suddenly awakened to new dedication during some crisis in life.

The unevenness of Christian growth is a part of human imperfection and a problem to those who try to teach discipleship. Impulsive action and double-minded attitudes often mar discipleship.

The graces of the Christian life assume a steady continuity. A reliable and disciplined Christian can be described by words like loyalty, integrity, mercy, justice and maturity. Steadfastness keeps faith strong, even as we are kept by the God who is faithful to us.

But how can imperfect men, who strive for this gracious life obtain the balanced and steady growth that is required? This is achieved only by disciplined living.

Giving Oneself

A crucial example of impulsiveness and discipline is seen in the incident when Jesus asked his disciples to identify him. Their confession was to be the culmination of Christ's training of his disciples. Now, by the Sea of Galilee, before going to Jerusalem for the last time, he would see if they really understood who he was (Matt. 16:13–28). Simon Peter showed divine understanding in his answer: "You are the Christ, the Son of the living God." But his spirit was not disciplined to accept the consequences of what he had said. He even grew bold and rebuked the Lord for speaking of his coming death in Jerusalem. Like many after him, Peter made an instantaneous confession of faith without any consideration or understanding of the discipline that must follow.

Peter's all too-human error may be one reason that, after Peter's confession, Jesus charged the disciples to tell no one that he was the Christ. The disciples did not yet know what it meant to speak of him as the Lamb of God who would take away the sins of the world. Only a few days before this confession, they had related Jesus reference to "the leaven of the Pharisees" to actual bread. At that time, Jesus had rebuked them for their little faith. "Do you not yet perceive?" he asked. For men of such small perception to speak openly of the Christ would have added more confusion to the multitudes who already had so many answers to Jesus' question, "Who do men say that I am?"

Previously, Jesus took occasion to teach his disciples what responsible commitment to him would involve: "If any man would come after me, let him deny himself and take up his cross and follow me" (v. 24).

This giving of oneself has been continually emphasized in writings on discipleship by Dietrich Bonhoeffer and others.

How did Jesus persuade others to give themselves and to become involved in his work and purposes?

He captured men's attention. This was not done by wearing a bizarre costume or by performing daring feats of bravery. It was accomplished through the natural channels of human speech and hearing. Jesus spoke truth with authority. He answered the everyday questions of men. People stopped and listened. Crowds gathered. Enemies argued, were frustrated, and went away saying: "No man spoke like this man speaks."

He captured men's imaginations. Men saw beyond themselves. Here was no self-interest like that which absorbed the Pharisees. Here was one who even defied them and dared to involve himself with ordinary people—even to the extent of self-denial and self-sacrifice. When the common people heard Jesus, more than his words entered their thinking. Their imaginations were freed from pervasive guilt and liberated to think of dignity, justice, and mercy. They felt his love. They were filled with hope.

Jesus gave men responsibility. His disciples heard his truth and, with enlightened imaginations, declared him to be the Messiah. But Jesus wanted a man to be a responsible disciple—responsible for his words of commitment and responsive to Jesus' purposes. So he set forth certain requirements: "Let him deny himself, take up his cross and follow me" and "feed my sheep." The disciples were made responsible for sharing themselves, their knowledge, and their understanding of Jesus' teachings. And we, like they, find our highest self-fulfilment in doing this. Imperfect men become new men in Christ.

A disciple must understand something about sacrifice and discipline before he can be a reliable witness. It is not enough to be enthusiastic, to speak quickly, to obey any good impulse.

"Father of the Bride" was a popular movie about impulsive parents who wanted to offer their very best to their married children. The bride's parents-in-law drew up plans for a new addition to their home so son and daughter-in-law could live with them. The mother of the bride was in a contest with the mother-in-law to furnish the nursery and thus gain control of a grandchild.

Only the father of the bride restrained the impulses of self-centered love enough to let the purposes of a new marriage find fulfilment. He saw that the young couple must make their own decisions. Gently and firmly he helped them to resist the pressure of possessive middle-aged people. The daughter turned to him and cried, "Oh, Daddy, you are the only one who understands."

After the father of the bride had "given his daughter away"—really a part of himself—he accepted the consequences of his action. His child no longer belonged to him; she was the woman who was to be one flesh with her husband. This was part of the disciplined wisdom that made this father delightful. And who does not rejoice in the mother who can love her child and still release her?

Accepting Correction

Simon Peter's love for his Master was sincere, but it was an impulsive affection. Jesus had to continue training his disciples so they would follow *him* instead of following their own ideas or emotions.

Why must the impulsive, irresponsible expression of love be corrected? Because, as Reuel L. Howe has pointed out in *Herein Is Love,* love may be misled into a possessive, patronizing, or an impetuous situation. Any of these distort the true purpose of love, which is to do good to others as Christ has done for us.

Possessive love contains the element of self-interest. In *Look Homeward, Angel* a mother dominates her grown sons and deceives herself into thinking that she cares only for their best interest. As her oldest son dies, the mother clings to his hand while others try to draw her away. In despair, her youngest son calls, "Mother, *let go.*"

But Mother cannot "let go." When the younger son receives money from his father to go to college, the mother cannot tell him good-bye, and release him. Instead she makes statements calculated to increase his feeling of guilt and to defeat his motivation for an education. She was willing to destroy his career in order to keep him close by.

The antidote for this "smother love" is self-restraint. The parent restrains his inherent impulse to hold and control a child in order to release the child to make some choices for himself and, thereby, to develop.

The parent, the professor, the pastor, the friend must say like John the Baptist, "He must increase, but I must decrease." We must willingly limit our domination over another, constrain our desire to live another's life for him.

Self-denial is the only way to keep the mature respect and independent admiration of those who once depended upon us. The parent who denies himself and willingly supports son or daughter in independent decisions will find that he has gained the lasting affection of his children. But those who cling possessively to a loved child lose it either through smothering its self-identity or by driving it away in rebellion. "It" is used intentionally, rather than he or she, for possessive love does not know another person as "thou." The child, the pupil, the parishioner is an "it," an object on which a dominant person grows his own ambition, or a dependent person nourishes his own life.

Love can also take a patronizing form. This happens when we are unable to understand how others feel. We assume that, since we wish to do good to others, they will automatically rejoice over our goodness. When they do not, we feel rejected and disappointed. Why were they not grateful for our beneficence?

We are resented when we do not give *ourselves,* when we care for others only as objects of our charity. We "do good" to a person with no thought about how we would feel if one day we should be in the same situation.

The cure for patronizing love is Christian humility. We are to bear one another's burdens. But we need always to consider that we also might have been tempted to fall or to be in conflict, even as our brother may have been (Gal. 6:1–5).

Paul teaches that we are to bear the burdens of others and also to bear our own load. How can these two be reconciled? In humility, we bear the burdens of others and our own as we see that we also could be disgraced, defeated, dependent people. We minister to our brother even as we ministered to ourselves at some earlier (or will later) time.

Love, as in the case of Simon Peter, that expresses itself impetuously, sentimentally, and in sudden urges, often creates suspicion and cynicism. Some persons may believe our rush of good words. Out of their desire for help, they may be seduced by our quick offer of friendship that produces no abiding helpfulness. When it is time to bear the burden in the heat of the day—to repeat the same kindness again and again, to meet defeat and return with encouragement—then the good impulses fade away. We are too busy. We are sure they do not wish our help any more. We tried to do what we could, and they would not receive us.

What would we really be willing to do for another person over a period of time? Late in the 1950's, a social scientist went to South America to see if a sense of self-respect could be restored to a group of peasants. From time to time, well-wishers had made brief visits and had preached a few sermons against the annual drunken festival of the natives. But no lasting program of self-help had been established.

But this time help was offered for a definite period—four years. The only requirement was that the natives were to develop their own leadership, with the assistance of American advisors. A hometown boy who had moved to a neighboring city, came back to become the first leader for his people in their effort against poverty. Within a few years, the natives had learned new agricultural methods, had organized a movement to buy their land from absentee owners, had organized an annual fair at which they displayed their newly-learned crafts. After a few years, the guidance team returned to an American university and reported the change in the annual festival. In the past, it had been a drunken orgy because the people had no hope. Now with a sense of pride in their craftsmanship the festival had become a joyous celebration among people who enjoyed the products of their own land.

During the 1960's, persons in many countries have said that they did not know what American people were really like until the young people of the Peace Corps came to their countries. This comment might well make American Christians in their own hometowns ask: "What do other people think we are really like?" Can we talk about Christ's love then allow a state legislature to cut off all assistance to poverty stricken mothers who have illegitimate children? Do we help in times of voter registration, or do we just talk about democracy? Do we keep our friendship with those who are divorced or who have lost their position in society?

How often do our own words deceive us into thinking that we love others? "He who looks into the perfect law, the law of liberty, and perseveres, being no hearer that forgets but a doer that acts, he shall be blessed in his doing" (James 1:25).

Continuing Development

People who are honest feel very dissatisfied with themselves when faced with the questions that have just been raised. The apostle Paul recognized that we do not do the good that we should do, and we fall into evil that we would like to prevent. Who can rescue us from this dilemma? Only the Holy Spirit. He, by his constant presence can make possible a life of moral obedience. (Rom. 8:2–17).

What kind of fulfilment is possible through the Spirit? Certainly, there is an enrichment of personality—but not a replacement. We remain persons with the same talents, but we use them with a different attitude. Self-sacrifice, humility, and steadfastness are qualities that increase rather than obliterate our personalities. We are more real, more lovable, more "filled with the Spirit." This is the abundant life. This abundance produces enthusiasm, not emotional excess. The apostle Paul warned the Corinthian church about "speaking in tongues."

There are reasons for people sometimes loosing themselves in these excesses. They may be so frustrated by the degrading conditions under which they live, or by the deprivation of personal affection, that pent-up emotion must be expressed. In such cases the real cause for concern is not the occasional explosion but the pattern into which the pieces of personality fall in the following weeks and months.

Or, a person may be excessively emotional because he is loosely put together. His early training was chaotic. There was no opportunity for him to learn self-restraint.

In some churches, an emotional explosion may occur after years of formalism. People have been given no opportunity to express themselves emotionally, to let others know that their religion matters in relationships with one another.

The "fruit of the Spirit" touches the heart as well as the head. But, by tradition, Christian expression is more in the direction of disciplined living than in emotional expression. Paul describes love, joy, peace, long-suffering, kindness, goodness, faithfulness, meekness, self-control as the fruits of the Spirit (Gal. 5:22f.). The gift of the Spirit gives men guidance and hope for godly living despite their imperfections. It provides freedom from sin. It leads men from self-deceit to free knowledge of self, from impulsive and irresponsible actions to gracious consideration for the impact of their attitudes and actions upon others.

Prayer, personal relations, Bible reading, meditation, self-discipline, the fellowship of worship—all are channels for the flow of God's gracious Spirit.

But always there is more. Christ has redeemed us out of the present evil age, yet the New Testament writers continually remind us that full redemption is yet to come (2 Cor. 5:2; 2 Peter 3:13). Knowing his imperfections, and trusting in the Spirit, the disciple waits and watches. The Spirit of Christ is within him, but the fulfilment of Christ's kingdom is yet to come. The earthly career of Jesus has pointed the way. The Holy Spirit is our counselor, but the reign of God is not sovereign in our lives or in ways of the world about us. The reminders of this coming time in the sayings of Jesus are numerous indeed (John 5:28–29; 6:39–44; 12:48; 14:3).

As the Lord taught again and again, a watchful disciple is a more obedient and faithful servant. His ever-present expectancy of the Lord's return is one motivation for righteous action. What would we do if the Lord were to return today? A watchful disciple should be living and acting the same way he would if the Lord should tarry. He has enough guidance for today. If his life is filled with the Spirit, he needs only to look at the present in the light of what will be in the future. Hope in the Lord's return is not meant to paralyze us but to perfect our faithfulness.

Some day the mortal will become immortal and the imperfect will be made perfect. In the presence of Christ's Spirit, there is grace for today and hope for tomorrow. This is the motivating power for a transcendent ethic in a human disciple.

9

The Process of Transformation

The findings of Luther Buller, presented at the beginning of the last chapter, led to a discussion of the steadiness of Christian growth. This is the discipline of discipleship.

Types of Growth

But there are dimensions of growth to be considered other than slow versus spontaneous.

Inclusive vs. compartmentalized.—Inclusive growth is the ideal for discipleship. Each part of the personality is progressively penetrated by the spirit of Christ. A mature person considers what his Christianity should mean in his home and in his business. He evaluates his cultural and racial assumptions by the same standards he uses for judging his equals. He thinks of the problems of people in other lands as he would those of his own community. He expands intellectually, emotionally and socially.

This ideal growth can be stunted in several ways. Sometimes our culture compartmentalizes Christian love. A missionary, who had returned from the Far East, told of a couple from the country he had served who attended the same church that the missionary did after they all were settled in the States. One day the Oriental husband sought out the missionary and told him that a fellow employee had said to him, "Be good." He had looked in the dictionary under "be" and "good," and could not see how the two were related. He had asked another Oriental what the words meant and was told that this might be a warning about his homelife which, at the time, was showing some strain.

The missionary commented that the phrase "be good" was just an American expression of good will, but that there might be something about the Oriental's home life to be explored. The husband said that his wife was depressed. She saw American women shopping and heard them talk of going places with their husbands, but she enjoyed none of these things.

"Perhaps," said the missionary, "you, even as a Christian, are still treating your wife in America as though you were in a Buddhist land." This had never occured to the husband. He had been good to his wife in the tradition of his homeland and had not considered the different needs she might now feel among the emancipated women of America.

Many an American man could learn, as did the Oriental gentleman, that his wife has special needs. Such a man is considerate of others on social occasions. On the job he cooperates and helps fellow workers. But at home he often seems like a different person. Of one husband, his wife said: "I dread to see Saturday come. He lies around the house, unshaven, glum, and won't do a lick of work. I have to sweep up around him." A man who is habitually gracious at work and grouchy at home has not yet grown up enough to see that love demands the same attitudes everywhere.

And what of the wife who demands that her children obey every teaching of the church but requires them to "come inside" when the children of divorced, Jewish, or Catholic parents appear in the yard? She thoroughly believes in daily Bible readings but sees no relationship between what she reads and the intolerance she teaches her children. Here again, Christian love is compartmentalized. The woman grows in intellectual faith but without feeling for others.

Among young people, the ideal of inclusive discipleship can be inhibited by traditional religion, by parents, or by society. "They don't want us to study anything new" is a common complaint of the youngsters. Emotional maturity is encouraged, but not intellectual investigation. When young people read critical studies of the Bible, or a different theology, or about "new morality," adults are often alarmed. One Sunday School teacher reported to her pastor: "I just couldn't stand that freshman tearing the Scriptures to pieces. I gave him a piece of my mind, and I don't think he'll disturb our class any more." Sure enough, the young man, home from college for the summer, disturbed the class no more. He dropped out, found friends outside the church, but still came to the preaching services.

Conscious vs. unconscious.—In conscious growth the individual knows his deficiencies, makes specific plans to overcome them, and sees evidence of failure or success as he tries to be a disciple. Typical examples of this type of growth would be the religious rituals discussed in a previous chapter. Here are activities that can be measured. In these ways a person knows if he has kept the faith.

But the deeper attitudes—the fruits of the Spirit—are not so easily observed by the self. In fact, the growth of humility would be inhibited if a person continually looked for evidence of it! The self-forgetfulness of a disciple so naturally leads him to service that he seems unconscious of it. And, as we saw earlier, he is more winsome because of his unawareness. If someone were to praise him, he would be skeptical of their judgment, for he does not consider himself that highly.

The Direction of Change

To maintain this self-forgetful attitude in adulthood certainly is not easy. American culture rewards secular success, material achievement, self reliance, assertion of talent. If a man is to succeed in business, he certainly cannot be a wallflower. Or, if he is to be respected in a profession, he must assert his judgments. The man who knows the people who have power and who will play up to them soon will be on top himself, especially if he also has some talent to match his ambition.

This search for success is so all-pervasive that few persons seem to understand how sacrifice and suffering could ever be related to church membership or community service. In one Sunday School class a man was heard to say: "Really, this lesson about suffering is beyond me.

How can a person go wrong if he serves God? I know that I've prospered since I began to serve him." The man was neither boastful nor arrogant; he was stating a self-evident truth to which most members of the class gave assent.

These men were middle-aged. They had made the necessary compromises to get ahead. But some of them could probably remember earlier years when it was not so easy to serve both God and mammon. Dr. Richard McCann found that in early maturity there is a real struggle between the self-assertiveness of adulthood and the self-forgetfulness taught in childhood by pious parents.

As children, we learn that Christians are to think of others rather than themselves. The direction of our lives is to be toward others. We are to love, forgive, give up pleasure for the sake of those in need.

But soon the world teaches us to "give up childish things." Friends tell us to look out for ourselves. Older persons advise us to push for this or try for that. Wives berate their husbands for not "getting ahead like other men," and husbands are disappointed when wives do not look as glamorous or well-dressed as the wives of other men in their income bracket.

It is quite a jolt for an idealistic young person to discover that people are expected to be "good" until they are out of high school. Then they are to be "able" when they get jobs and make their way in the world. One young man received his awakening in his own church. For years he had heard and believed that a Christian renounced self. He had refused invitations to "worldly amusements," witnessed to classmates who withdrew from him, and generally felt "good" because this was the way a Christian was expected to act.

All went well until a Negro tried to join the church. Then the pastor explained the need for waiting, to accommodate the feelings of older people. When this young man went with others in his group to ask for an "open door," the pastor replied: "All things are not expedient. We must not destroy our fine church organization because of something like this. People would be offended."

"But, but–" stammered the young man, "you're the one who has preached for years that we must deny ourselves, give up everything for the sake of our faith. Now you say we can't admit a man on the basis of his faith alone because some people would be offended. I think you have one standard for those of us under twenty-one and another one for yourself."

These words of an angry young man vividly portray the conflict which young people face in many areas of life as they move from the benevolent orientation of childhood into the adult world where competence and assertion are prized—even in the church.

The Ability to Change

The young man was angry because a pastor and others could not face opposition for the sake of Christian principles. Let us look beyond anger to the reason why some people can move ahead despite the crowd, while others wait until it is safe before they change.

From a psychological point of view, the first person to

step out in a new direction is probably the most adequate person in the crowd. He is the individual who received enough love and assurance as a child that he doesn't need too much reassurance as an adult. He can stand a good deal of frustration and opposition; he considers it "just one of those things."

In contrast, a person who was insecure and rejected in earlier years will look upon frustration as just one more evidence that no one really loves him. Hungry for affection, he cannot stand more deprivation and may sell his soul to anyone who will offer him some attention or security. This is the follower, not the leader, in new ways of life.

Sometimes we meet a very self-assertive person who was frustrated in childhood. He seems to be a leader in new things, but is without assurance and poise. Instead, he assures himself by force and domination that he is important. When others do his will, he feels secure.

The more adequate person is not too interested in whether or not others follow him or approve of him. So long as he can present his own views graciously and has opportunity to move in ways that satisfy him, he is content. This is a rather self-contained way of life rather than self-assertive. For examples of such persons see chapter 12 of the book *Motivation and Personality* by A. H. Maslow.

These are psychological dimensions of change. What about the spiritual? Is an adequate background the only requisite for the person who yearns to make the grade, or is there divine grace that can fill in the emotional gaps?

The self-actualized person—the "ten talent" man—needs the discipline of Christian faith to discover higher, deeper, nobler values than secular culture can ever present to him. Without such values he may easily become complacent about himself and contemptous of others. Discipleship saves him from self-stagnation and pride. And, it gives him an unattainable goal that can satisfy every new dimension of a creative life.

On the other hand, the deprived, inadequate person has a terrible time taking a first step toward change and staying with it. For such persons, God's grace seems so far away, yet it is so necessary. Many have found adequacy in their discovery of God as Heavenly Father, Christ as Saviour, and the Holy Spirit as guide. These persons have found that "when mother and father forsake me, then the Lord will take me up." They know the failures of their lives and a despair so great that only a divine intervention—salvation—can stir hope and refresh their souls. And in the maze of their self-doubts and overburdened consciences, they have found a guide for their true selves—the Holy Spirit. He is one on whom they can depend, and he provides an inner source of motivation. This refreshing spring welling up in them is a source of strength for imperfect disciples. He replaces the deprivation that the normal relations of life failed to provide.

How does the Spirit move? We have discussed one—internally. He moves also in the powerful channel of interpersonal relationships—with parents, friends, associates, teachers, and pastors. Much has been written in psychology about the importance of therapeutic environment that is necessary for change in personality to take place. But there exists something beyond the group. One person comes out of suspicion and hurt to risk himself in group discussions, while another continues to interpret every remark as hostile. The ability of one person in such a group to become more Christlike, despite his background, is one of the surest evidences that life can be transformed. This is the confirmation of faith—that what we see take place in human personality is a sign of a creative, living personality beyond ourselves.

Notes

1. Eduard Schweizer, *Lordship and Discipleship* (Naperville, Ill.: Alec R. Allenson, Inc., 1960), p. 20.

2. Alfred Friendly, "The Better War—II," *Washington Post,* January 31, 1966, p. A-1.

3. Roy W. Fairchild and John Charles Wynn, *Families in the Church: A Protestant Survey* (New York: Association Press, 1961), pp. 184–89.

4. Philip Stern, "The Unexpected Dividend," *The South Today,* ed. Willie Morris (New York: Harper & Row, 1965).

5. Abraham Maslow (ed.), *New Knowledge in Human Values* (1st ed.; New York: Harper & Row, 1959), pp. 4-5. For other examples see Samuel Southard, *Pastoral Evangelism* (Nashville: Broadman Press, 1962), chaps. 8-9.

6. Jonathan Edwards, *Religious Affections,* ed. John E. Smith (New Haven, Conn.: Yale University Press, 1957), chap. 1.

7. Gerhard E. Lenski, *The Religious Factor* (Rev. ed.; Garden City, N.Y.: Doubleday & Co., 1961).

8. Mark 6:41; 11:11; 14:22-23; Luke 24:30; 4:16; John 7:14; 10:23.

9. Mark 1:35; 6:46; Luke 3:21; 5:16; 6:12; 23:34,46; Matt. 11:25-26; 26:39-42; 27:46.

10. *Ritual in Family Living* (Philadelphia: University of Pennsylvania Press, 1950).

11. Eric Berne, *Games People Play* (New York: Grove Press, 1964).

12. Washington Gladden, "O Master, Let Me Walk with Thee," *Lyric Religion, The Romance of Immortal Hymns,* ed. H. Augustine Smith (Westwood, N.J.: Fleming H. Revell Co., 1931). Used by Permission.